Effective Speaking at Work

A Practical Route to Improving Your Communication Skills in a Professional Environment, Becoming More Charismatic, and Empowering Productivity in an Effective Way.

Milton Jamison

© Copyright 2021 by Milton Jamison. All right reserved.

The work contained herein has been produced with up-to-date relevant knowledge and information on the topic described in the title for entertainment purposes only. While the author has gone to every extent to furnish up to date and true information, no claims can be made as to its accuracy or validity as the author has made no claims to be an expert on this topic. Notwithstanding, the reader is asked to do their own research and consult any subject matter experts they deem necessary to ensure the quality and accuracy of the material presented herein.

This statement is legally binding as deemed by the Committee of Publishers Association and the American Bar Association for the territory of the United States. Other jurisdictions may apply their own legal statutes. Any reproduction, transmission or copying of this material contained in this work without the express written consent of the copyright holder shall be deemed as a copyright violation as per the current legislation in force on the date of publishing and subsequent time thereafter. All additional works derived from this material may be claimed by the holder of this copyright.

The data, depictions, events, descriptions and all other information forthwith are considered to be true, fair and accurate unless the work is expressly described as a work of fiction. Regardless of the nature of this work, the Publisher is exempt from any responsibility of actions taken by the reader in conjunction with this work. The Publisher acknowledges that the reader acts of their own accord and releases the author and Publisher of any responsibility for the observance of tips, advice, counsel, strategies and techniques that may be offered in this volume.

Table of Contents

Introduction 6

Chapter One: Basic Communication 10
    Defining Communication 10
    Communication in the Workplace 12
    Communication's Four Basic Steps 14
    How a Message is Sent and Received 19
    Chapter One Overview 27

Chapter Two: How To Talk To Anyone About Anything . 30
    Reasons Why Your Workplace Communication Isn't Working.. 30
    Effective Communicators 33
    Casual Conversations 36
    Verbal Communication When Talking To Anyone About Anything 38
    Chapter Two Overview 43

Chapter Three: Effective Communication For Strong Working Relationships 47
    Workplace Facts and Statistics 47
    Poor Communication In The Workplace 48
    Solutions To Poor Communication 49
    Managing Tough Conversations To The Best Of Your Ability 52
    Chapter Three Overview 54

Chapter Four: Effective Communication For Morale 57
    Workplace Morale Basics 57
    Indicators of Poor Employee Morale 58

Chapter Four Overview 63

Chapter Five: Effective Communication For Productivity 65

Workplace Productivity Basics 65

Workplace Productivity Facts and Statistics 65

Workplace Productivity Tips 67

Face-to-Face Interactions Also Help Increase Productivity 71

Chapter Five Overview 73

Chapter Six: Effective Communication For Online Work 75

History of Online Work/Video Conferencing 75

Online Work Communication Options 75

How to Make Sure Your Company's Online Work Is Successful . 77

Be Careful With Humor 79

What It Takes To Have Successful Online Employees 80

Chapter Six Overview 84

Chapter Seven: Effective Communication For Company Growth 86

Communication Within An Ever-expanding Company 86

Communicating While Expanding Tips 87

Chapter Seven Overview 93

Chapter Eight: Effective Communication For Stellar Management 95

Communication Begins With Upper Management 95

Tips For Upper Management 97

Tips For Great Management Communication 99

Pleasing Employees 102

Denial In The Workplace 103
Our Ever-changing World And How Communication Fits In ... 103
Chapter Eight Overview 105
Conclusion 106

Introduction

Congratulations on purchasing *Effective Speaking at Work*. As we all know, communication is now a complicated art, science, and liability, especially in the workplace. Understanding the full spectrum of communication is vital to every word we speak. No matter who we are, professionally or personally, our words have to be delivered and received with great understanding, sensitivity and accuracy.

Communication in the workplace involves much more than simply conversing. Sixty percent of companies lack an internal communication plan, claims a Workforce study. Knowing the basic rules of communication is crucial to every conversation you have. No matter what your personal or professional role is in life, you must adjust your words in a way that works best for you and the communication you have with each employee. Your verbal and nonverbal communication can be adapted to meet each new hire's needs, each happy or disgruntled employee, owner, department manager, and even a partner, old friend in-law, and more. That's the beauty of communication. Your verbal and nonverbal communications genuinely reflect who you are and what you think.

Quality workplace correspondence relies on various factors, the most crucial being accuracy, staff engagement, and sufficient information message. Because we assume these facets of a message are easy to convey, we create a lot more misunderstandings. The original reason why people initially communicated was to make their needs known. While time has changed, rearranged, expanded, and even confused this process, somewhere, at the bottom of each word we communicate is still to make our needs known.

Our choice of words and how we say them can make or break our workplace relationships and opportunities. For good or bad, our words and actions reflect what we think and how we feel every minute of every day. That's the beauty, and the beast, of communication. The beauty is in the words that make love come alive, gratitude spread, and poetry sing. The beast is in the liability of saying the wrong thing. Tokyo Olympic Organizing Committee Chairman, Yoshiro Mori, had to resign after saying, "Having more women on sports association committees would lead to longer meetings because of their competitiveness and the need to make their voices heard." Currently, nearly everything we say is put under a continual microscope. This book teaches you how to avoid, if not eliminate, this type of situation.

Developing a winning communication style does not mean you have to memorize catchy phrases or quotes from great orators. Essential communication means assessing your current type of workplace communication, understanding the tried and true basics of sending and receiving messages, then adjusting the way you deliver your messages at work. Once you do this, you will have:

- More Influence
- More trust
- More understanding
- More satisfaction
- Less conflict

When it comes to communication:

- 7% of our message is the words we choose (verbal)
- 38% of our message is the tone we use (nonverbal)
- 55% of our message is the body language we choose (nonverbal)

There are all types of mediums in place to make sure your message is received. These include verbal, such as emails, individual exchanges, meetings, and texts, both formal and informal. A SaneBox study conducted by Workforce found that 62% of employee-received emails are not essential. Yet, an Adobe study found that office employees spend more than five hours daily checking and answering their emails.

Effective Speaking at Work guides good communicators to become great communicators at work and beyond. *Effective Speaking at Work* shows you how to talk to anyone about anything. Also included is information on expressing yourself safely in an ever-changing world of challenging communication because what we say does matter.

Babe Ruth once said, "The way a team plays as a whole determines its success. You may have the greatest bunch of individual stars in the world, but if they don't play together, the club won't be worth a dime."A business team works the same way. Too often, upper management will treat their clients like gold and then turn around and treat their employees like garbage, which is why Babe Ruth's words are well worth remembering.

Too many books focus on word choice and not enough on our nonverbal communication. However, study after study proves that nonverbal influences, such as tone and body language, are equally, if not more important. The benefits that come from stellar communication skills are limitless. And this isn't because the focus is on you. This is because you have put your focus on others. Through this process, you will receive more joy in each workday that ends up creating more joy in your life and the lives of those around you. Thank you for choosing this book. Make sure to leave a short review on Amazon if you enjoy it. I'd love to hear your thoughts. Now, **let's get started.**

Chapter One: Basic Communication

Including time spent at work, home, and play, the average American currently speaks around 2500 words per day. That's more than enough words to make our needs known or possibly get us into a heap of trouble.

When it comes to communication, know that one of this book's goals is to adhere to Plato's saying, "Wise men speak because they have something to say; Fools because they have to say something."

Hopefully, at work, home and play, we'll always land nicely in a positive exchange of words.
That's what this book is all about.

Defining Communication

Dictionary.com defines communication as "the imparting or interchange of thoughts, opinions, or information by speech, writing, or signs. If only workplace communication was this easy, we'd never have any misunderstandings and have a lot more forward movement. Yet, too many owners, upper management, and employees believe communication is just an exchange of thoughts and opinions, which is why so many misunderstandings exist in the workplace.

There's a story about a monk who entered a monastery where he received stringent rules. The monk accepted the vow of silence, which meant he could not speak, not even one word. However, there was one exception to this rule: every year, each monk was allowed to say two words.

After being in the monastery for one year, the monk was allowed to say his
first two words at a meeting with the head monk.

It has been one year," the monk said, "What are the two words you would like to speak?"

"Bed hard," said the monk.

"Thank you," said the head monk.

The following year, the monk again attended the annual meeting where the head monk said, "It's been one more year. What are the two words you would like to speak?"

"Food awful," said the monk.

"I see," replied the head monk.

Another year passed, and another annual meeting arrived.

The head monk once again asked the monk, "What are your two words that you would like to say this year?"

The monk said, "I quit!"

"Well, I can see why," said the head monk. "All you've done since you've been here is complain."

This is the perfect example of workplace communication that will send your employees right out the door to new employment elsewhere.

There is much more to communicating with your employees effectively than simply exchanging words. Employees want to express the workplace needs that will help support them on their journey to help your company achieve success. Once heard, they need to experience the most critical step in workplace communication: follow-up.

Continuous variables go along with each word we speak. No two conversations are ever the same because of the verbal and nonverbal cues included. Bringing all these variables into play makes it easy to see how strong the focus must be to create effective workplace communication. Communication unlocks life and creates more room for understanding, appreciation, and courage.

Essential communication takes ordinary life, work, people, and relationships to the extraordinary. Basic communication eliminates most misunderstandings, even if it is just the mere act of taking the time or taking more time to communicate effectively and listen. Or, it might be less communication in a more effective way.

Communication in the Workplace

Too many companies hold lengthy, meaningless meetings filled with poor communication over every issue that wastes company time and money. Adapt to the times. Most employees prefer instruction along the way, as needed, rather than taking time away from their workday to group and discuss company needs. Yes, some meetings are appropriate and a must. However, many company issues can be addressed as they arise.

Take a look at these facts:

- Organizations and companies who have effective communication programs in place outperform their competition by 3 to 5 times.
- According to a 2014 Gallup Poll, one of the most significant changes in recent decades has been how Americans communicate.
- As the world becomes small through social networking, communication becomes more vital.
- Effective communication is more necessary as our lives, emotions, actions, and reactions become more exposed through social networking.
- Communication has now, more than ever, become a vital tool for survival and coexistence.
- Erasing addresses, cities, and countries, the need for high-quality communication is not only a luxury but essential, particularly in our critical environments.

The other reason why gaining effective communication is a must in the workplace is to keep up with the changing world of verbal and written exchanges. For instance, work environments have become much more informal as we now refer to our bosses by their first name, casual Friday is commonplace, and couches now replace cubicles. Slack messages have replaced meetings, as have texts and emails. A new study by IE business school in Madrid suggests that formal meetings with set agendas and required attendance are more efficient and accurate in reflecting all aspects of the company. However, the most preferred method is still on-the-spot discussions rather than formal communications and meetings.

As we move forward in a more fast-paced world, thanks to up-to-the-minute technology, so much more continues to change, all through the avenues of communication. Before the technology boom, there was no other way to expedite the information process than hold a meeting. Any other way, tied up the phones with no way to accommodate multiple-line meetings, and notes arrived by hand. Formal meetings were the fast-paced resource for their time. As in all things, computers have sped up disseminating information in the most effective way possible.

Communication's Four Basic Steps

With so many variables influencing everything we say, the fact that we understand anything at all is impressive. Again, this confirms why having a deep understanding of basic communication skills is a must. The four critical components included in essential communication are:

1. Encoding (what you say to another person)
2. Medium of transmission (the way your words are transmitted)
3. Decoding (how the other person decodes your words)
4. Feedback (the other person's response to your message)

To break this down further:

Encoding - Encoding begins when an owner, manager, or employee begins their message. This message includes both verbal and nonverbal input. The responsibility for the communication starts with the sender. Within this encoding process, the sender must include some factors for this step to be successful. The sender's message usually consists of attitude, expectations, and knowledge. The sender uses certain symbols, as in words and gestures, to convey his or her message so that the receiver will understand precisely what the sender is trying to say. Then, like a human-computer, the sender "pushes the send button." From this point, the receiver receives the message. The receiver's brain then decodes the message, translating it into concepts and ideas the receiver has collected over their life experiences. This is why thinking about the other person is so important. To be a successful communicator, you have to think about what you're going to say based on what the other person thinks and feels before speaking your first word. This is called empathy. The more you feel for your listener, the more your listener will relate to what you say. This essential tool, once practiced, will automatically become part of all your communication processes and help you communicate with anyone anywhere.

Medium of transmission - This is the form in which the sender sends the message. The message could be delivered verbally or written, through a phone call, a text message, zoom, or sign language.

Decoding - This happens when the receiver receives the message. This part of the process is where someone could draw an imaginary line between the sender and the receiver as the sender loses control of the message and it enters the receiver's brain. Interpreting the message can be subjective because so many variables influence this part of the process. Possibly, the receiver had a bad day or is too busy to listen or does not like you. This is where the sender's word choice and nonverbal messages become so important. Mutual understanding happens when the sender's encoding and medium of transmission are interpreted correctly by the receiver. The receiver's and the sender's processes are not that much different. What is different are all the life experiences, beliefs, and opinions the sender has collected in their life and brought into the conversation. This is why word choice and mutual empathy are so important.

Feedback - This represents the end of the communication exchange. Feedback happens after the message is received and decoded and then offers feedback. Or, the receiver does not respond, which is also considered feedback.

Here is an example of what happens when the encoding, medium of transmission, decoding, and feedback process breaks down:

Encoding: You have an employee who wants to bake a cake for another employee's birthday. The only thing she needs is the ingredients. Her manager said he was going to the store to pick up a few items for the employee break-time refrigerator. So, she asked if he would pick up the cake ingredients, so she could bake the cake in the company kitchen when he returned.

Decoding and Feedback: The manager heard what she said, then offered his feedback: "I will go under one condition. I have a meeting in a half house, so I can only pick up enough items that I can check them out in the 10 Items Or Less lane.

She **decoded** his message then offered her **feedback**: The employee heard what he said and laughed. "That'll be too easy."

She quickly wrote down her **encoded** short-list and gave it to the manager. He left, and the employee expected her manager to be back soon.

All is good, correct?

Time passed and, still, the manager had not returned to work. The employee started to worry, so she found the grocery store's phone number and was about to call when she heard her manager's car pull in the company driveway.

Out of breath, the mangered entered the workplace carrying three bags. He hurriedly placed them on the kitchen table.
"I'll be right back with more," he said in a hurry and rushed out the door.

The employee could not figure out what happened. She gave him a list with only seven items.

The manager came back, set the bags of groceries on the counter and started to unload them. There was a pound of butter, a couple of bags of sugar, and a few bottles of vanilla in the first one. The second bag held dozens of eggs. In the third bag, there were lots of packages of lard and her grocery list. That's when she figured out what happened.

When the manager said he needed to go through the express lane, she numbered her list of items, one through seven, to make sure she had less than ten items. Her list looked like this:

    1 pound of butter
    2 bag of icing sugar
    3 bottle of vanilla
    4 dozen eggs
    5 lard
    6 big bag of flour
    7 large cartons of milk

Bringing in the six big bags of flour and seven large cartons of milk, her manager said, "I couldn't go through the express lane because when I read (decoded) the message, there was so much stuff that I had to go through the regular checkout. It wasn't until I was on my way home that I realized the mistake I had made. When you listed each item #1 thru #7, I thought those numbers referred to the amount of each item I should buy."

They both had a good laugh, knowing sometimes communicating is like that.

Accurate communication only happens when the four basics steps to communication are followed every time, and when clarification is requested for any words that may seem unclear.

One of the most critical places for accuracy is within the healthcare system. Estimations are that a clinician conducts as many as 150,000 patient interviews during a typical career. Can you imagine being accurate through all those interviews? Patient interviews are the most frequent procedure the clinician performs. However, communicating with a patient receives far less training than other clinical courses. Evidence continues to show that a proper approach to this clinical procedure improves healthcare of the patient measurable.

Other facts surrounding this vital communication exchange show that:

- The majority of the decisions related to patient diagnosis comes from the time spent with the patient hearing his or her medical history.
- Patients rarely have enough time to tell the story of their current medical condition.
- Interruptions during the clinician and patient visit can result in diagnostic inaccuracy. ,
- When interruptions happen, the patient begins to believe that their story is not essential and becomes hesitant about explaining the rest of their story.

- When patients are interrupted, collecting vital information is impeded, as is the relationship.

For this particular study, the subjects were doctors and patients. However, if the participants are managers and employees, the results are nearly the same.

How a Message is Sent and Received

When it comes to basic communication, Professor Albert Mehrabian--known for his studies on verbal and nonverbal communication--discovered the following:

Spoken words amount to 7 to 10 % of communication - What this means is that because words make up such a small part of communication's impact, the sender must choose each word wisely. Words are one of the most powerful things we own. Use them for good, and you'll have no regrets later. All communication can be mutually understandable if you follow the basics. The words we say tell who we are. Words make dreams come true. Words can make or break us. Is there anything more powerful than words? Many adults have spent years in therapy because of the bad words they received from others. Yet, many people have also excelled because of words received from people who made sure their empathetic messages were well-structured.

Word Choice

When it comes to word choice, you might want to ask yourself and your employees:

- Are you choosing the best words to fit the best communication you need at the time, every time?

- Do your words create an openness to have a mutual exchange between you and the receiver?
- Do you say words that are hard to understand, or are you speaking over the receiver's head, possibly to show you are more important than them?
- Do you use offensive language or derogatory words?
- Do your words include more words about the other person's interests rather than your own?

The tone of voice comprises 30 to 38 percent - When it comes to communication, our tone says more about how we feel than the words we choose. There is an art to combining word choice with tone. Once mastered, ineffective communication becomes much more effective.

Yes, words carry some weight, but the tone has three times more. The tone is becoming more vital because of voice-only techniques, like Podcasts. The standard interpretation of the choice of tone includes:

- Deep tone = maturity, trust, often used in advertisements.
- Extremely deep = dark feeling
- Firm and confident = distinguished, important
- Quiet tone = weak, awkward
- High tone - lacks credibility
- Well-defined = clearness of thought
- Unclear = deceiving or confused
- Exacting = narcissism
- The pace of breathing = indicates personal life pace

Many times, we are oblivious to our tone. If, while speaking, you receive constant negative feedback, you might want to consider exploring your tone.

Some additional nonverbal contributions include:

Empathy - One of the most critical aspects of communication is having empathy for the receiver. This means feeling from their perspective as well as yours. Empathy is the ability to feel emotion for another person. As established in Stephen R. Covey's book, The Seven Habits of Highly Effective People, "Seek to understand, then be understood." No conversation should ever occur without the art of feeling where the other person is coming from while engaged in a conversation. Like the old joke, "My wife says I lack empathy, but I don't understand why she would feel that way." One way to develop instant empathy with the other person you are speaking to is to ask questions to understand the other person first. This will give you the tools you need to address the conversation from a healthy perspective.

Validation - Even something as extreme as PTSD (Post Traumatic Stress Syndrome) receives comfort from simple validation and understanding words. And, an Alzheimer's patient also calms down with simple words of validation. When people in dire situations receive words of encouragement frequently, they make better choices. Employees are no different. This is why mirroring back their words is so important. Hearing their own words back means they've been heard, which is very validating.

Context - The words that precede or follow a specific word in a sentence often support its meaning? The context of a message is the environment in which the message is sent, including all the words in the surrounding sentences and where the words were physically delivered, as in a court of law or a phone call or a casual conversation over dinner. Context also includes the history between the people communicating and the positions in life the two people hold. The thoughts and experiences leading up to the conversation are also part of the context. Also included are the participant's beliefs, values, opinions, and lifestyles that influence the message's interpretation. Context also consists of the relationship between the two people. Are they friends? Boss and employee? Husband and wife? Each one has its own set of expectations. And temperament. What is the mood of the people talking, and what led up to the conversation? Context can either clear up a misunderstanding or confuse it.

To help keep the context of a conversation in proper perspective, the following is helpful:

Calmness - keeping calm after sending or receiving a communication, especially when the message is unclear. Calmness between both the sender and the receiver can help clear up the confusion more easily.

Openness - making sure both the sender and the receiver are open-minded leaves a lot of room for proper assessment and faster understanding of what is being said and heard. Quantified Communications' survey showed that, on average, among 100 workers, 17 hours are spent weekly trying to understand misunderstood messages, costing a company $525,000 in productivity per year.

To listen - Epictetus, a Greek philosopher who was a slave as a youth in Rome before gaining his freedom around 60 AD, once said, "'We have two ears and one mouth so that we can listen twice as much as we speak." Even that far back, people were trying to work on learning how to communicate a message.

Another example of listening happened between Sherlock Holmes and Dr. Watson while on a camping trip. After a delicious meal, they decided to call it a day and go to sleep. While laying there a few hours, Holmes woke up and tapped Watson on the shoulder. "Look up and tell me what you see."

Watson replied that he saw millions of stars.

"What does that tell you?" asked Holmes.

Watson thought for a minute, then said, "Astronomically, this means there are countless galaxies and possibly billions of planets. Astrologically, this tells me that Saturn is in Leo. I'm thinking, horologically, the time is quarter past three. And theologically, this means that God is all-powerful, and we are mere beings in an infinite situation.

Holmes took this all in and said, "No, Watson. What this means is that someone's stolen our tent!"

One situation, two experiences. Holmes listened and then redirected Watson to the correct path before them.

Nonverbal communication (body language) equals 55 to 60 percent - nonverbal communication comprises the most significant percentage of message conveyance and yet receives the least attention. You could be delivering Martin Luther King's "I Have a Dream," but if your nonverbal communications are not in sync, your speech might send out a message you never intended for the receiver to hear.

Nonverbal communication comprises an endless variety of behaviors, from a smile, a frown, a scowl, a nod, the shaking of one's head, a gentle touch, a wink, two thumbs up, or even a combination of these, to name a few. While verbal communication is happening, nonverbal communication either supports, complements, or distracts and even confuses the receiver. Knowing nonverbal gestures is vital in understanding what might be the true meaning behind someone's words. Some of the most common gestures include:

- Erect posture = confidence
- Scowling eyebrows = anger
- Leaning forward = interested
- Relaxed stance = openness
- Stiff stance = defensive
- Slumped posture = depressed
- Hands on hips = aggression
- Tapping or drumming fingers = impatience

Another point to remember when conversing with others is the distance you should use when carrying on a conversation. Included is the standard for the United States and a few other countries:

- The United States is 24 to 36 inches
- Argentina is 30 inches
- Romanian is 55 inches
- Saudia Arabia = 39 inches

By reading all the cues involved in the communication, you will determine how to be the most effective. Mutual consideration is so important, as both the sender and the receiver pay as much attention to one another as they do to their contribution. The Mckinsey Company, an advisory firm, found that employee connectivity is one of the most critical workplace communication goals. By doing this, employee productivity increases by 20 - 25 percent.

When it comes to communicating in the workplace, you must avoid some words:

- Hate
- Never
- Always
- You (when discussing another person's negative qualities),
- Must
- Can't
- Swear words

Many people have taken the time to pass along their beautiful words of wisdom when it comes to communication:

> The most valuable of all talents is that of
> never using two words when one will do.
> *Thomas Jefferson*

> The six most important words: I admit I made a mistake.
> The five most important words: You did a good job.
> The four most important words: What is your opinion?
> The three most important words: If you please.
> The two most important words: Thank you.
> The one least important word: I
> *Anonymous*

> Be careful of the words you say,
> Keep them short and sweet.
> You never know, from day to day,
> Which ones you'll have to eat.
> *Anonymous*

> A word is dead
> when it is said,
> some say.
> I say it just
> begins to live
> that day.
> *Emily Dickinson*

> Words—so innocent and powerless as they are,
> as standing in a dictionary,
> how potent for good and evil they become,
> in the hands of one who knows how to combine them.
> *Nathaniel Hawthorne*

When it comes to choosing the right words, choose them:

- Wisely.
- With the receiver in mind first, he or she will receive your words well.
- So they are clear and precise, not vague ones like, "I need you to do this over there."
- Using enough words to convey your message, but not so many that you confuse your message.

Not that you need to read the Thesaurus all day, yet this might not be a bad idea. The larger your vocabulary, the more words you have available. This will help get your message across correctly and help you adjust no matter who you are talking to and what subject you are discussing.

Current trends include having more critical, tactical conversations that also include more meaningful and productive messages.

Companies and personal communicators are seeking more trust and interaction, as well, including having:

- A mutual understanding that leads to more equally satisfying relationships.
- Shared goals in the workplace, home, and community.
- More trust as reflected through transparency.
- More working together to achieve an equal and better life for all.
- More two-way communications that involve more listening.
- More answers to questions that remain misunderstood.

Chapter One Overview
Communication's Four Basic Steps
1. Encoding (what you say to another person)
2. Medium of transmission (the way your words are transmitted)
3. Decoding (how the other person decodes your words)
4. Feedback (the other person's response to your message)

How A Message is Sent And Received
- Spoken words amount to 7 to 10 % of communication
- The tone of voice comprises 30 to 38 percent
- Nonverbal communication (body language) equals 55 to 60 percent

When It Comes To Word Choice:
- Do your words create openness to have a mutual exchange?
- Do you say words that are hard to understand or speaking over the receiver's head?
- Do you use offensive language or derogatory words?

- Do your words include more words about the other person's interests rather than your own?

Tone includes:
- Deep tone = maturity, trust, often used in advertisements.
- Extremely deep = dark feeling
- Firm and confident = distinguished, important
- Quiet tone = weak, awkward
- High tone - lacks credibility
- Well-defined = clearness of thought
- Unclear = deceiving or confused
- Exacting = narcissism
- Pace of Breathing = indicates personal life pace

Some nonverbal contributions include:
- Empathy
- Validation
- Context
- Calmness
- Openness

Companies and personal communicators seeking:
- An understanding that leads to more equally satisfying relationships.
- Shared goals in the workplace, home, and community.
- More trust as reflected through transparency.
- More working together to achieve an equal and better life for all.
- More two-way communications that involve more listening.
- More answers to questions that don't make sense.

Some of the most common gestures include:
- Erect posture = confidence

- Scowling eyebrows = anger
- Leaning forward = interested
- Relaxed stance = openness
- Stiff stance = defensive
- Slumped posture = depressed
- Hands on hips = aggression
- Tapping or drumming fingers = impatience

The distance you should consider when carrying on a conversation:
- The United States is 24 to 36 inches
- Argentina is 30 inches
- Romanian is 55 inches
- Saudia Arabia = 39 inches

Chapter Two: How To Talk To Anyone About Anything

Communication has evolved through the centuries: From smoke signals to hieroglyphics to carrier pigeons, morse code, newspaper, radio, telephone, television, computer, and the internet, communication will evolve as the world becomes more complex and people want to be heard. Making connections with anyone anywhere, including the workplace, means understanding the timeless and universal basics of communication, as discussed previously.

Successful workplace communication happens when we assess our current style of expressing ourselves, refresh ourselves with the tried and true basics of communication, and then apply these changes to our relationships and contacts. Once these simple steps find a place in our heart and mind, a lifetime of stellar communication is automatically ours with memories of endless awesome conversations rather than needing to call back and apologize constantly.

Talking to anyone about anything means you are prepared to speak to someone happy or sad. Within this range of conversations, following the basics, along with a few more tips, can help you succeed.

Reasons Why Your Workplace Communication Isn't Working

One reason is that too many work environments experience information overload and do not recognize this as a problem. The number one reason for a messy, chaotic home environment is because there are too many items that are not disposed of in a timely manner. This can be anything from junk mail to old clothes. The workplace environment functions on the same principle. If time is not taken to get rid of files, equipment, and information that's no longer needed, all of this excess interrupts streamline information, products, and services that are the most important piece of company productivity. Get rid of the old and bring in the new. Everything that exists in your company must be a vital part of your company's objectives, or it must be removed and put somewhere else. This includes communication. Too often, companies use outdated programs, save favorite techniques and stick with the way things have always been done. This type of mentality is unable to keep up with the times. Communication must include only the latest and greatest approaches to exact and timely communication. Your employees will thank you.

Too many companies start believing that communication is so important that they develop too many ways to communicate and messages start getting duplicated, sent to the wrong employee, and the whole process becomes confusing. Decide what type of communication you want to use and stick to it.

Another problem is that there isn't a solid chain of communication command in place, and messages get sent to the wrong person. This can slow down productivity if not cause the whole process-to-completion factor to fail.

Informing employees of information they don't care about and withholding information they do care about is another common issue. Most vital communications include company:

- Acquisitions and divestments
- Competition
- Goals

- Growth
- Strategies
- Structure
- Performance
- Mission statement
- Vacation, illness, and other types of Paid Time Off
- Values

Too many companies don't take into consideration the type of employees they hire and how to meet their communication needs. Are your employees analytical, creative, rigid, outdoors, loud or quiet? From coroners to restaurant servers to ski instructors, seamstresses, chefs and more, each workplace environment and employee style must be considered.

Workplace communication is the most crucial factor to consider. Employees want to have a voice, as in:

- Being involved
- Encouraging others
- Building trust
- Learning what's needed
- Helping others
- Driving curiosity
- Support meaning
- Build enthusiasm
- Empower each other
- Instill purpose
- Improve conditions
- Raise engagement
- Improve the brand

Communication is one of the soft skills required by companies, and most managers do not feel they have the skills to communicate with their employees, and the majority of employees would agree. This is one of the main reasons why workplace communication struggles and includes:

- Confusing directions.
- Not enough time spent communicating with employees.
- Do not communicate routine recognition of employees.
- Often take credit for employee ideas.
- Criticism is not constructive but damaging.
- Never talk to employees about anything other than the company.
- Don't even know what their employee's names are.
- Don't take enough employee surveys to find out what is and isn't working.
- Don't celebrate achievements.
- Workplace environment is all business and no play.

If more companies understood the lifeline communication is, they would set up a strong system in the beginning and work daily to maintain it.

Effective Communicators

So, how do we make sure our words are adaptable at work and with anyone you meet, whether at work or at play? The answer comes from our parents' first words taught us when we were young: think before you speak. Even more importantly, learn the Four Basics of Communication before you speak. Learn how communication works, brain-to-brain, so you are skilled at taking these steps before you begin a conversation. As Mark Twain said, "It usually takes me more than three weeks to prepare a good impromptu speech."

Whether at work or elsewhere, effective communicators do not speak only about themselves or show everyone they are the expert on every subject. Instead, they consider how the receiver feels and spend the rest of their time listening. Effective communicators enter every conversation with an empathetic mindset, a feeling of equality, and that everyone has value. They are also open to new thoughts and feelings for the sake of mutual awareness and understanding.

Whenever the basic skills of communication are used, more extraordinary conversations follow. Some of the most positive words you can use in conversations include:

A person's name - Using this tactic only in positive conversations, people love hearing their name. Not overdoing it with name usage, but letting them know you recognize who they are and that they are valued. There is a difference between saying, "How're you doing?" and "How're you doing, Kent?" No other word is more relatable to a receiver than positively hearing their name.

Yes - Studies have shown that saying "yes" at the beginning of a conversation is more likely to send that conversation into a positive zone. In the sales industry, saying "yes" three times in one conversation can increase the closing rate from 18 to 32 percent. This doesn't mean you have to say "yes" to everything that comes up, but having an "I can do" attitude goes far in the workplace.

Help - Helping shows that you are a team player and sends the message that everyone is moving forward together. Helping a coworker when they ask is called "reactive helping." Perceiving that a coworker needs help is called proactive helping. Surprisingly, studies have shown that reactive helping is more effective than proactive. Reacting generates more gratitude between both the giver and the receiver.

Thank you - Gratitude is the icing on the communication cake. And gratitude is contagious. Can you imagine the morale boost after the Campbell's soup CEO wrote and sent out 30,000 thank you notes? Southwest Airlines uses appreciation as its number one morale booster. Voted America's #13 Best Employers of 2018, Southwest Airlines goes out of its way to send cards to employee's children's graduations, marriages, and family medical issues. The best way to generate workplace satisfaction is to begin words of gratitude at the top.

But – This tiny word is powerful but negative. "But" negates the first half of any sentence, which is usually the complimentary half. "We appreciate all your hard work, but..." Whenever the word "but" is used, this word becomes the focus of the sentence. When "but" is replaced with "and," the message is cohesive and receives a more positive reaction.

Why – Why is a great question to ask, as it often is by doctors in an emergency room. In a work environment, "why" should only be used positively. Otherwise, it can become offensive and create a defensive response. Used correctly, "why" can suggest taking a deeper look into something.

In the Buddist religion, relationships are considered to be like mirrors, reflecting certain things about ourselves as we converse. This being the case, take a look at yourself the next time you communicate. See if your choice of words, tone, and body language are appropriate for the topic and the setting. And avoid making every conversation sound like you're in the middle of a five-alarm fire.

Casual Conversations

Everyone has engaged in casual conversation, small talk, ice breakers, chance meetings, and water cooler exchanges. These conversations may not change the world, but they are essential parts of our life as we try to stay connected. The fun thing about communication is that there's a lot of room for appropriate adventure once you know the basics.

Anywhere you talk to people, even while networking, make adventure part of your communication. Instead of relying on the standard questions, like "Hi, how're you going? What do you do for a living?" Don't stop there. Ask questions that will help you get to know the person, like what they like most about and least about their job. Are they in the field they desired? If not, what would be that field? Everyone has fantastic stories they hold inside. Seek to find out what those stories are.

Whether you are at work, home, or a party, casual conversations are an integral part of everyday life. Asking a yes or no question results in a yes or no answer. Most of us automatically know how to answer the most common questions continually asked, like those that arise at a company party. To steer away from being the vanilla ice cream of communicators, follow Albert Einstein's observation, "The definition of insanity is doing the same thing over and over again," and ask different questions.

Also, remember to never engage in a conversation for one-upping the other person. For example, have you ever shared a medical issue with someone, and the first thing they say is, "Well, you think that's bad..." You know you're in for a verbal sport of one-upmanship. One-upper can't help themselves. But, as a manager, you must resist this urge to ever engage in this rude sport. If not, you and your words will quickly become uncomfortable, annoying, and even toxic. One-uppers are triggered by both happy times and times of suffering and figure this as a time to shine. Nothing could be further from the truth. The opposite of communication empathy is one-upping. It is selfish, self-centered, and negatively reflects on the person and the communication.

Instead, your job as an employee or manager is to learn as much as you can about your employees. The more the other person is allowed to speak, the more they will walk away and remember you as a great person.

Other tips you must remember when talking to anyone about anything are to:

Avoid ridicule or making fun at someone's expense - If a joke is only funny to the person delivering it, then the joke is just not funny.

Don't try to be everything to everyone - Be yourself. People see right through other people, so they know when you're phony instead of having a real interest in making a genuine connection. Mark Twain called it right when he said, "A man's (or woman's) character may be learned from the adjectives which he habitually uses in conversation." Your employees will get to know a lot about you by what you say to them, and this is a good thing

Do not fear silence - Silence can feel awkward, but it is also a respectful pause as you regroup to say meaningful things. Silence can mean acceptance of having another person in your space. When it comes to silence, the nonverbal communication that goes along with it helps to move your conversation forward. In other words, if you sweat, this means you're nervous. If you pause with a comfortableness about you, you will convey comfort. So, don't let silence paralyze you. Let it be your friend. Mark Twain once said, "The right word may be effective, but no word was ever as effective as a rightly timed pause."

Verbal Communication When Talking To Anyone About Anything

Verbal communication is the opportunity to make your most important message understood. Choose the most transparent, most accurate words to convey your message. Determine the pace of your conversation and the tone of your voice. Make your message for the receiver to receive and interpret correctly. Since encoding, or communicating verbally, is first in any conversation, the following are some more of the basic elements of verbal communication:

Volume - Most people are unaware of how loud, or soft, they sound. In a study by Albert Mehrabian, tone, including volume, accounts for 38 percent of all messages. The simple act of making sure your volume is appropriate increases the receiver's ability to trust you and confirms your credibility. Unless you are a singer or professional spokesperson, you probably don't have access to equipment that monitors your volume.

You know your volume is too high in the workplace when:

- Your employees assume you're mad.
- Employees believe you're probably hard to communicate with.
- The employees judge you before they even know you.
- Employees tend to focus on your volume rather than your message. You've been told repeatedly to dial it down.
- Once you stop talking, you notice the silence in the room.
- You laugh loudly too.

- You'll never win a whispering contest.
- You're on the phone, and everyone knows what you're talking about.
- Your employees can hear you before they see you.
- You talk even louder when you see or hear something you like.
- You have an inner voice that also causes you to overshare.
- Employees believe you're borderline too straightforward.

No worries. Sometimes, even something as simple as recording yourself on your cell phone while involved in a casual conversation can give you a clue as to how loud or quiet your volume is. Possibly, your voice is too big for most discussions. One study suggests volume can indicate if a doctor has been sued for malpractice by how he speaks. Doctors who have been sued speak louder. A loud volume can appear to the receiver as if the sender lacks empathy, understanding, and indifference. One tip on volume suggests that, when in doubt, take on the receiver's volume. This makes it easier for the receiver to understand and accept the message.

The Director of Speech Acoustics Lab, Dr. Amee Shah, at Cleveland State University, discovered some interesting facts about speech volume:

Your size might indicate your loudness - Bigger larynxes and thicker vocal cords usually belong to larger people. And most men talk louder than most women. Is this the case with your volume?

Age impacts your volume - The older you are, the stiffer and slower your vocal cords become, the quieter your voice is. Could this be true with you?

Childhood influence - If you were raised in a large family or around someone who was hearing impaired, possibly you were introduced to speaking louder so you could be heard. The opposite is also true.

Learning to speak at the right volume can be learned. If you want to change your volume, ask others to help you by requesting that they tell when you are too loud or too soft. Take their advice and even ask a friend to signal to you if your voice is getting too loud.

Inflection
According to a University of Chicago study, a person's ear can distinguish 1,378 different tones. Compare this to the fact that our eyes recognize only 150 color hues. This means hearing is nearly ten times more sensitive than eyesight. This same study found that revealing how you say something is five times stronger than what you say.

Voice inflection differs in each person, and every person develops their intonation:

- A flat tone reflects a lack of interest, boredom, or indecisiveness.
- A pitch that goes from low to high, specifically when using a vowel, indicates a question, patronization, surprise, or suspense.
- A pitch that drops from high to low, specifically within a vowel, adds power, confidence, finality, and certainty to your message.
- A low tone is often used when stating facts or closing a deal.
- A genuine low inflection takes practice to acquire.

Word Emphasis

Whether intentional or not, emphasis on a word or phrase changes the sound of a sentence. Different ways of emphasizing a word, or set of words, include:

- One word over another
- The first syllable of a word
- The keyword in a sentence
- A nonverbal pause
- A nonverbal gesture

The sender brings attention to a specific verbal or nonverbal communication so that it becomes the central focus. By contrasting one word or gesture against all the others, the sender hopes the receiver will understand the conversation's direction. Whenever a person emphasizes one word, there is usually a reason why: concern, fear, excitement, anger, or some other emotion. Make sure you highlight the right word, or you'll confuse the receiver as in these common examples below:

- CONflict, which means an argument or disagreement, and conFLICT, means two stories that don't agree.
- SUSpect, a person who's possibly guilty of a crime, and susPECT means assuming that something has happened a certain way.
- PERfect meaning having reached a state of perfection, and to perFECT means to be in the process of achieving perfection.
- REcall means returning a product to a company because of a flaw, and reCALL meaning to remember.
- OBject meaning an item, and obJECT as in disagreeing with something that's been said in a court of law.

Pace

As mentioned, the general rule for pacing is to match your pace with the receiver's pace. Everyone has their own pace for speaking or the words they speak per minute or words per minute (wpm). Following are the average speech rates for:

- Presenter: 100 -150 wpm
- Average conversation: 120 - 150 wpm
- Audiobook voice: 150 - 160 wpm
- Radio Hosts/Podcasters - 150 - 160 wpm
- Auctioneers - 250 wpm
- Media Commentator - 250 - 400 wpm
- Fastest talker: 637 wpm
- The average speaker - 150 wpm

When it comes to pace, there are a few methods you can use to see if your speed is appropriate:

- Does the conversation feel comfortable between you and the receiver?
- Does the receiver seem agitated as he or she listens?
- Is the receiver reading your lips to help understand what you are saying?
- After calculating your words per minute, is your pace within the normal range?

To calculate your words per minute:

1. Use your cell phone
2. Talk for one minute
3. Convert your speech to text
4. Cut and paste the text into a word counter.
5. Total words/number of minutes = words per minute.

Other Tips for Improving Your Verbal Skills
1. Remember, the last voice you hear is always your own. You are the final interpreter of all that you hear and experience. This interpretation becomes your view of your life. These thoughts determine what you think about yourself, your goals, beliefs, opinions, desires, and more. Because of this, your thoughts determine how each of your communications will be executed.

2. When the decoding process of message and interpretation match, this can be the most potent communication form. One example of this is two people who fall in love.

3. On the other hand, when two people exchange differing thoughts, a verbal argument results if the decoding process repeatedly breaks down. The reason for this is both parties are not aware of or do not want to incorporate the basic rules of communication into their lives.

Chapter Two Overview
Effective Communicators:
- Think before they speak.
- Have empathy.
- Say the person's name.
- Say, "Yes."
- Offer help.
- Say, "Thank you.
- Pay attention to yourself while you communicate.

While Engaged In Casual Conversations:
- Avoid ridicule or making fun at someone's expense.
- Don't try to be everything to everyone.
- Do not fear silence.

You know your volume is too high at the workplace when:
- Your employees assume you're mad.
- Employees believe you're probably hard to communicate with.
- Your employees judge you before they get to know you.
- Employees tend to focus on your volume rather than your message.
- You've been told repeatedly to tone it down.
- Once you stop talking, you notice the silence in the room.
- You laugh loudly too.
- You'll never win a whispering contest.
- You're on the phone, and everyone knows what you're talking about.
- Your employees can hear you before they see you.
- You talk even louder when you see or hear something you like.
- You have an inner voice that also causes you to overshare.
- Employees believe you're borderline too straightforward.

Other facts about volume:
- Size might indicate loudness
- Age impacts volume
- Childhood influence determines the volume

Inflection:
- A person's ear can distinguish 1,378 different tones.
- How you express something is five times stronger than what you say.
- A flat tone reflects a lack of interest, boredom, or indecisiveness.

- A pitch that goes from low to high, specifically when using a vowel, indicates a question, patronization, surprise, or suspense.
- A pitch that drops from high to low, specifically within a vowel, adds power, confidence, finality, and certainty to your message.
- A low tone is often used when stating facts or closing a deal.
- A genuine low inflection takes practice to acquire.

Word Emphasis:
- One word over another
- The first syllable of a word
- The keyword in a sentence
- A nonverbal pause
- A nonverbal gesture

Average WordPace:
- Presenter: 100 -150 wpm
- Average conversation: 120 - 150 wpm
- Audiobook voice: 150 - 160 wpm
- Radio Hosts/Podcasters - 150 - 160 wpm
- Auctioneers - 250 wpm
- Media Commentator - 250 - 400 wpm
- Fastest talker: 637 wpm
- The average speaker - 150 wpm

Tips to see if your pace is appropriate:
- Does the conversation feel comfortable?
- Does the receiver seem agitated?
- Is the receiver reading your lips?
- Is your pace within normal range?

To calculate your words per minute:
1. Use your cell phone
2. Talk for one minute
3. Convert your speech to text
4. Cut and paste the text into a word counter.
5. Total words/number of minutes = words per minute.

Other Tips for Improving Verbal Skills
- Remember, the last voice you hear is always your own.
- When the message and interpretation of the message match, this is the most potent communication form, as in two people in love.
- When the decoding process repeatedly breaks down, a verbal argument is the result.

Chapter Three: Effective Communication For Strong Working Relationships

When it comes to communication in the workplace, where does the responsibility most often rest? On the shoulders of the managers, employees, both? Consider this true story:

"I had a manager once who at every one of my performance reviews said I had to work on my communication skills. He even kept sending me to classes on communication. He said I wasn't very polite or wise about the workplace environment. He said I lacked empathy and wasn't a good listener. Despite all of his criticism, I tried to learn and grow because I like my job. This manager eventually left the company, and when a new manager came in, he kept saying to me, "I don't know why anyone would say you have a communication problem. Your skills are just fine with me."

Workplace Facts and Statistics

When it comes to effective workplace communication, consider these statistics:

- 20 to 25% of increased employee productivity happens when employees are connected.
- 2.5 hours a day are spent on employees looking up the information they need to do their job.
- 62% of emails received in the workplace are considered useless.
- A study conducted in 2009 by the Communication Insight Center found that effective communication in the workplace produced 47% more revenue over five years.

How important is effective workplace communication? Consider these facts regarding some powerful moments in the workplace, yet the employees didn't think before they communicated:

- A wrong comma in a contract cost the Rogers Company $2 million because it was placed incorrectly and accidentally canceled the deal.
- On July 17th, 1981, because of poor communication between the project managers and the engineers, 114 people were killed, and 216 suffered injuries in the collapse of two walkways in the Hyatt Regency Kansas City Hotel.
- Pepsi has made four times more writing mistakes than Coke in its posts on Linkedin.

Each of these examples shows a lack of preparation for a vital communication moment. On the other hand, these few simple words, well-thought-out, changed the world:

- "Mr. Gorbachev, tear down this wall." President Ronald Reagan
- "I have a dream that one day this nation will rise and live out the true meaning of its creed, 'We hold these truths to be self-evident, that all men are created equal." Dr. Martin Luther King
- "That's one small step for man, one giant leap for mankind." Astronaut Neil Armstrong

Poor Communication In The Workplace

Poor internal workplace communication can negatively impact a company with low morale and high employee turnover. Even worse, poor communication can have a long-term effect on a company's bottom line. From a 2018 study by Arthur J. Gallaher & Co., long-term workplace communication processes are non-existent for 60%

of companies. Low morale and high turnover are usually the result. Also adding to the difficulty is that this type of poor communication environment affects new employee attraction.

Some of the most common substandard communication processes include:

1. Continuing to use outdated methods, like memos, faxes, and printed messages.
2. Overstuffed emails that employees have to scan through to find the vital points.
3. In most instances, interoffice phone calls, unless a vital discussion is necessary.
4. Face-to-face messages, unless a vital discussion is necessary.

Solutions To Poor Communication

More and more companies are switching to mobile communication, like Google workplace, and Slack. These programs also help with nontraditional employees, as in those who work remotely, freelance, or are contract-based.

Too many companies still focus on external strategies for their customers yet neglect to develop their internal communication strategy. However, the more inferior the quality of communication is within a company, the poorer its quality is with its customer. A business's communication strategy can only be successful when a strong inner voice is established, and a solid external voice is also a top priority. This fact alone can paralyze a company that seeks to have customer loyalty.

Understanding what's at risk when a company does not make internal communication a top priority is usually the motivation needed to change. Here are some questions to ask when it comes to building a new internal, successful communication strategy:

- What are all of your current internal communication processes?
- Which processes are effective and which are not effective?
- What are the most effective ways your employees buy-in to top-level management?
- In what ways could you encourage more employee engagement?
- How can you become more mobile-friendly?
- How can you engage disconnected employees better?
- How can you create a culture that values employee communication?
- In what ways could you more effectively inform employees about advancement opportunities?
- What practical ways could you communicate with employees about issues that affect the business and the industry?
- How could you communicate changes in policies and procedures?
- What would be the best way for your employees to be notified about company goals?
- How could you foster efforts to have more employee contribution to company goals?

After establishing the most effective internal communication system for your employees, there are other ways to build on vital, positive employee interactions:

Casual conversation - As a coworker or manager, engaging in casual conversation with your coworkers can give you and the company a chance to get to know your employees beyond what they wrote on their resume. This is a vital practice for many reasons:

- To find out what employees could add talents to the team.
- To learn the personalities that make up the team.
- To discover fascinating facts that make each employee unique.

Those managers who do not believe casual conversation in the workplace are productive because they could be missing something important. Not only do you learn about possible valuable office resources, but casual conversation also brings the team together in, hopefully, a more reliable way. Thinking to eliminate small talk in the office will allow more time for working couldn't be further from the truth as company morale suffers, isolation sets in, and boredom follows. For those who believe this, you would do well to post a sign in your office that says, "Stronger Together."

Employees who discourage casual conversation miss the strength and shared purpose of employees who band together because they feel a professional but emotional bond. People who know each other are more likely to help out when the going gets tough.

Casual conversation can also go downhill quick, so this type of communication must include a few ground rules to avoid pitfalls:

Workplace conversations should always be friendly and professional - No one wants to hear about the personal ups and downs of your life. Positive announcements are significant, here and there, but always pay attention to the TMI rule. You want your coworkers to walk away feeling better, not cringing.

Know when the conversation needs to end - Workplace conversations can go on and on and get in the way of workplace productivity. Remember that you are at work, respect this, give the casual conversation a time limit, and then move on. Typically, informal discussions should be no more than 10 minutes long, and the amount of time equal to a short break.

Never gossip, no matter how tempting the thought might be - The tried and true theory here is that if you are willing to talk about someone else behind their back, you are highly likely to talk about the person you are speaking to behind the back. Gossipers are gossipers, and anyone can become prey to this team- destroying communication.

Upper management interaction is beneficial - Bosses who interact with their employees will receive more support from their employees, which turns into increased productivity. Participating in conversations puts you in the mix. When employees share information and are willing to join in, employees feel more of an open two-way communication street. Thus, they will feel more comfortable offering necessary feedback and listening to vital communication that they need to hear and accept.

Managing Tough Conversations To The Best Of Your Ability

Like having to clean up spilled garbage, having to engage in a challenging conversation is never on the top of someone's fun-to-do list. However, a company is only as solid and impressive as its behaviors at the lowest level of a company's existence, so you must make sure that even these conversations are as positive as expected. Here are a few time-proven tips:

1. Get the conversation off to the right start by valuing yourself and the other person equally.

2. Try to express negative thoughts positively. It's okay to be frustrated. It is not okay to convey this disrespectfully. Sometimes the exchange will be about something that's not easy to talk about and will bring sadness or frustration or even anger into the receiver's life. Because you are the one who started the conversation, you are the one responsible for how the conversation goes. If the basic skills of communication were made for anything, it is this.

3. Think before you speak. This means pausing or even preparing beforehand what you are going to say in all your communications. Try to walk yourself through each conversation and anticipate any reactions.

4. Do not talk too fast or too slow.

5. Do not use too loud or too soft a volume.

6. Do not conclude. Do not use the "You" word. This word creates defensiveness in a hostile setting.

7. Allow the receiver to process the information.

8. Embrace the silence that may be part of the nonverbal communication required by the receiver's mind so that he, or she, can handle the information they have just received.

9. Be clear. Sometimes, we think the worst thing we can do is to be direct. However, in a negative situation, like firing someone, you need to be straightforward enough to make sure the message is clear. You do not want to be so direct that you cause further pain, but not being clear can prolong the pain. In this case, less is best.

Chapter Three Overview

When it comes to effective workplace communication, consider these statistics:
- 20 to 25% of increased employee productivity happens when employees are connected.
- 2.5 hours a day are spent on employees looking up the information needed to do their job.
- 62% of emails received in the workplace are considered useless.
- Effective communication in the workplace produced 47% more revenue over five years.

How important is effective workplace communication? Consider these facts:
- A wrong comma cost the Rogers Company $2 million because it accidentally canceled the contracted deal.
- Because of poor communication, 114 people died, and 216 suffered injuries in the Hyatt Regency Kansas City Hotel collapse.
- Pepsi has made four times more writing mistakes than Coke in its posts on Linkedin.

On the other hand, these few simple words, well-thought-out, changed the world:
- "Mr. Gorbachev, tear down this wall."
- "I have a dream."
- "That's one small step for man, one giant leap for mankind."

From a 2018 study by Arthur J. Gallaher & Co., long-term workplace communication processes are non-existent for 60% of companies. Some of the most common substandard communication processes include:
- Continuing to use outdated methods
- Wordy emails.
- Interoffice phone calls.
- Face-to-face messages.

Questions to ask when it comes to building a new internal, successful communication strategy:
- What are all of your current internal communication processes?
- Which processes are effective and which are not effective?
- What are the most effective ways your employees buy-in to top-level management?
- In what ways could you encourage more employee engagement?
- How can you become more mobile-friendly?
- How can you engage disconnected employees better?
- How can you create a culture that values employee communication?
- In what ways could you more effectively inform employees about advancement opportunities?
- What practical ways could you communicate with employees about issues that affect the business and the industry?
- How could you communicate changes in policies and procedures?
- What would be the best way for your employees to be notified about company goals?
- How could you foster efforts to have more employee contribution to company goals?

Casual conversations help:
- find out what talents can be added to the team,
- learn the personalities that make up the team
- discover fascinating facts that make each employee unique

Casual conversation must include a few ground rules:
- Workplace conversations should always be friendly and professional.
- Know when the conversation needs to end.
- Never gossip, no matter how tempting the thought might be.
- Upper management interaction is beneficial.

Here are a few time-proven tips:
- Value yourself and the other person equally.
- Express negative thoughts in a positive way.
- Think before you speak.
- Do not talk too fast or too slow.
- Do not use too loud or too soft a volume.
- Do not conclude.
- Do not use the "You" word.
- Allow the receiver to process the information.
- Embrace the silence.
- Be clear.

Remember:
- Fifty-eight percent of people trust strangers more than they believe their boss.
- Fifty percent of employees quit their jobs because of their manager.

Chapter Four: Effective Communication For Morale

Workplace Morale Basics

Each company's "emotional environment" reflects certain morale. When employees feel good about themselves and the job they are doing, management has succeeded in doing its job establishing and maintaining positive morale. Management cannot make an employee happy, but management is the most potent influence in the workplace environment. It is established with the help of stellar conversations and other communications.

Upper-level management can set the standard and establish high morale to recognize and reward managers and shift leads. The motivational encouragement at this level sets the tone on how your lower-level employees will be treated.

When those in leadership roles have confidence in their job assignments, they usually turn around and instill this same positivity in their team. When employees know the company's vision and feel safe in their position, morale is high, and this spreads to the rest of the group.

Employees love feeling part of a winning team. When morale is high, employees enjoy going to work and be part of this type of momentum. Instead of needing to talk themselves into getting up and going to work, employees with positive feelings possess unstoppable energy that motivates them to meet the company's goals and expectations.

In other words, whatever level of morale the highest-ranking member of a company establishes, the employees will follow. As the saying goes, "The mother sets the tone of the home," the manager also sets the workplace environment's tone.

Indicators of Poor Employee Morale

Just as stellar communication leads to high morale, ineffective communication results in low morale, including:

- Not enough, or ineffective, communication between employees and management.
- Absenteeism is above what's expected.
- Agitated behavior in the workplace
- An abnormally high amount of employee complaints about minor issues.
- Tension between employees
- Substandard work
- Reduced productivity
- Above-average complaints from customers
- More employee turnovers
- Unengaged employees are work meetings

With companies like Glassdoor rating the positivity of a company's culture, no one can afford to overlook morale.

Ways to instill high morale must start at the beginning of the new hire process:

1. Set your employees up for success from day one. This includes stellar training with fantastic dialogue that focuses on the employee.
2. Equip them with all the tools they need to perform their job assignment

3. Have a plan for online employees where communication is vital.
4. In all that you do, make sure you communicate at your most motivational level.
5. Welcome feedback. The best way to increase input is by supporting people to seek it themselves. Asking and receiving feedback is a fantastic approach to self-development. Nothing motivates people more than witnessing their progress.

Great company leaders allow employees' unique talents to create morale that is empowering during both good and challenging times. This naturally increases employee engagement and productivity. Effective managers don't demand high performance. They put value in people by discovering their natural talents and then seek out opportunities to utilize those strengths. Not only does this tap into a deeper, more intrinsic type of motivation for employees, but it also allows managers to increase the capability of their teams. This includes:

Expressing employee appreciation- What makes appreciation so powerful is that when it's contagious. By sending a quick thank you note or simply noticing someone's hard work, morale boosts immediately. Plus, regular recognition can alleviate some of the day-to-day tension that employees experience.

Remembering to communicate on a fun level, too - Seriousness has its place, but so does fun. Make sure to laugh and smile when communicating with your team. Find ways to bring more of your true self to work and look for ways to get to know your employees on a more personal level. When you bring more of your authentic self to the office, you become more relatable and approachable. When you let your teams know you're human, not just a leader, you communicate that you see them as more than only employees. When your employees feel supported and encouraged to do their best work, they can do so with confidence.

Not sweating the small stuff - Nothing kills workplace morale faster than a reactive, dramatic boss who negatively addresses everything. When a manager is uptight, your department's general stress level will skyrocket, and enthusiasm will plummet. When company rules are disobeyed, remember, your employees are watching how you react to these scenarios.

Smiling more - As a manager, you have to deal with a lot of stressful situations. This is one reason why maintaining a sense of humor is so important. Through you, employees learn to laugh at themselves. Always look for the humor in things, and encourage your staff to do the same. Even when you are fuming and ranting, you can always find something to lighten the mood. Make it a goal to laugh at least once in every meeting.

Promoting a healthy employee work-life balance - The opposite of this is employee burnout and no company can afford this. Burn out happens when there is:

- a lack of appropriate social support
- taking on a heavier load than is expected
- doing multiple job tasks for employees who are not carrying their load
- too much overtime
- lack of appropriate resources
- inadequate level of appreciation
- disrespect of employee's personal time

By making sure social support is present, employee loads are appropriate for their job description, no overtime, no emails or phone calls during employee's off-hours, employee morale goes up. This happens as you:

Develop company trust - Employee morale can only reach a certain level when trust is not in place, and this level of enthusiasm is not very high. After all, employees aren't likely to communicate or contribute if they don't feel safe expressing themselves honestly at work. According to a Slack study on the future of work, 80% of workers want to know more about how decisions are made in their organization, and 87% want their future company to be transparent.

Go beyond an open door policy - More and more companies are reaching out to employees to get inside their heads and find out how they feel, what keeps them there, and what, if anything, they would change. The result can significantly impact first-line employees as great solutions, fun activities are established, and new initiatives are incorporated.

Establish outside the office interactions - This includes off-site parties like bowling, sporting events, or movies. Picnics are also popular, as are lunchtime trivia games with prizes and family-centered parties. Do not be like David, who worked for an assisted living who held pot luck dinner parties for their pathetically attended employees. Why?

- First - management made attendance at the employee social event mandatory.
- Second - the event was on a Saturday with no pay.
- Third - there was an agenda:
    - 6 pm - Employees arrive
    - 6:15 pm - Mingling (joking, etc.)

- 6:30 pm - employees casually introduce families to one another
- 6:45 pm - eat
- (and so on)
      - Fourth - Employees were pressured to bring their families and children to this event with no children's activities. Get the drift?

Create inner-office stress relievers - These are also becoming more popular. This includes gyms, onsite childcare, plus physical, mental, and emotional wellness classes.

Have a newsletter - Yes, newsletters can cater to employee morale nicely. There's space to express appreciation, incentives, upcoming events, all on a positive note and employee-centered.

Perform random small gestures of kindness - Picture employees as if starved for attention and appreciation, and it is your job to "feed" them—a surprise diet Coke for that diet Coke lover. Any type of fun swag, gift cards, surprise lunches, bonuses, and other incentives easily excite employees.

Have morale-friendly policies - Have a policies and procedures book in place, but not one that is so upper management driven that the employees cannot even engage in its message. Avoid ones that micro-manage and add undue burdens to an employee's workload. Tokens of appreciation and treats are lovely but remember never to create a working environment that impedes growth. This includes pages and pages of negative information and demands, along with never-ending lists of what not to do.

Be an example of high morale - When all is said and done, the best way to generate high enthusiasm is to be an excellent example of positivity, hope, flexibility, patience, and everything else that exhibits high morale for your employees. As President Dwight D. Eisenhower once said, "The best morale exists when you never hear the word mentioned. When you hear a lot of talk about it, it's usually lousy."

Chapter Four Overview

Employees love feeling part of a winning team. When morale is high, employees enjoy going to work and be part of this type of momentum.

Indicators of Poor Employee Morale:
- Not enough or ineffective communication.
- Absenteeism above what is expected.
- Agitated behavior in the workplace
- An abnormally high amount of employee complaints.
- Increased tension between employees.
- Substandard work.
- Reduced productivity.
- Above-average customer complaints.
- High employee turnovers
- Unengaged employees at work meetings

Ways to instill high morale must start at the beginning of the new hire process:
1. Set your employees up for success from day one.
2. Equip them with all the tools they need to perform their job assignment
3. Have a plan for online employees.
4. Communicate at your most motivational level.
5. Welcome feedback.

Increase the capability of their teams by:
- Communicating how much you appreciate your employees.
- Communicating on a fun level.
- Not sweating the small stuff.
- Smiling more
- Promoting a healthy employee work-life balance.

Burn out happens when there is:
- a lack of appropriate social support
- taking on a heavier load than is expected
- doing multiple job tasks for employees who are not carrying their load
- too much overtime
- lack of appropriate resources
- inadequate level of appreciation
- disrespect of employee's personal time

Employee morale goes up when:
- Company trust is present.
- An effort is made to go beyond the open door policy.
- Outside the office, interactions are established.
- Inside the office, stress relievers are established.
- Newsletters are consistent.
- Small gestures of every kind are made.
- Morale-friendly policies are in place.
- High morale is exemplified by upper management.

Are you enjoying this book? If so, I'd be really happy if you could leave a short review on Amazon. It means a lot to me. Thanks.

Chapter Five: Effective Communication For Productivity

Workplace Productivity Basics

Workplace productivity happens when a specific task is completed within a particular amount of time. When productivity is maximized, business success follows. Famous businessman Richard Branson is a huge promoter that a business is only as successful as its employees.

You can have the best resources, supplies, work environment, latest technologies, and most creative ideas, but your business will not thrive and grow if you have poor-performing employees. In other words, if your employees are not productive, your company will not turn a profit.

The right employees must be hired first, with primary consideration given to their ability to positively and actively engage in productive dialogue. And then it is your responsibility to build upon this. Productivity needs to be at the forefront, with all communications remembering this word as the central consideration from which all communications flow. Knowing what improves and what slows down productivity is vital for any company, and poor communication can kill productivity faster than you can say, "Closing Our Doors For Good."

Workplace Productivity Facts and Statistics

Salesforce states that 86% of upper management and employees claim poor communication, followed by low-quality collaboration, as the number one reason for project and product failures.

To increase productivity, companies must empower employees with a knowledge-rich environment. In this way, employees feel their part in business development. Collaboration happens at the top level of management and then filters down to a company's employee level. All of this begins with stellar communication; however, 57% of employees claim they receive a lack of clear direction, with 69% of managers claiming they feel uncomfortable talking with their employees. In this area, there is a lot of room for growth. Fortunately, currently, technological companies realize this and have come up with unique products to alleviate this issue. Programs like Microsoft Lync, HipChat, Bootcamp, Kato, Redbooth, Wrike, and Campfire, to name a few.

When it comes to internal communication, the key to success is finding the right platform for your company's needs. With all the programs available, there is bound to be one that matches your workplace's style. Considering that 90% of internal communication is informal, take time to choose one that creates forward movement for your company.

A Gallup poll wanted to find out what employees experience when they work in a stellar work environment, so they asked, and these are some of the responses they received paraphrased:

- I appreciate knowing what work expects of me.
- Upper management makes sure that I have all the resources I need to get my job done.
- Work continually has opportunities for me to grow and advance.
- I love the praise and recognition I receive for the work I do.
- Upper management and my co-workers care about me as a person.

- My personal development is supported and promoted at my work.
- My opinion counts.
- I know and feel my work assignment input is vital because of my work's mission and purpose.
- Within our workplace environment, all my co-workers are equally committed to doing quality work.
- Some of my best friends are my co-workers.
- Upper management stays in touch with me regarding my progress and contribution.

Workplace Productivity Tips

Ways to generate maximum productivity include:

Only communicate accurate information - Anytime information is conveyed, all data should be correct, clear, and easy to understand. If not, employees become confused. When this happens, productivity is halted until a complete understanding of the task is understood. Increased confusion occurs when managers are confused. However, when an effective internal communication process is in place, all information needed to complete a task is available and easy to understand. In most businesses, employees cannot begin or complete a task without upper management's direction to meet expectations. You will do your employees a fantastic service by implementing a communication-friendly service. And don't hesitate to obtain input from your employees. Most employees want to complete their tasks but lack the necessary resources to do so.

Develop trust through open communication - Trust happens through consistent, ongoing exchanges that include updates, new awareness, changes in expectations, or any other valuable information that needs to be conveyed to employees. Trust generates an environment of shared support, and this is where productivity flourishes. On the contrary, substandard communication breeds mistrust and suspicion. This environment creates wasted hours on the clock as employees spend time keeping an eye on each other, not working together or sharing tasks, and needing more management.

Solid workplace communication is the best solution for eliminating micromanaging. As proper communication begins to prevail, trust rebuilds. As a result, workers learn to trust the systems in place, and maximum productivity begins to take off. Employees are now motivated to take on the top level of their productivity and feel encouraged to enjoy a learning environment. It's often said that knowledge is power. This is especially true with employee productivity. Employees love not only knowing what they are doing but why they are carrying out their duties. This always helps them feel like their tasks are part of a winning process and not just something they have to cross off their list of responsibilities for the day.

Empower employees to become experts in their field - By informing them of all aspects of their productivity tasks, they take on "pride of ownership" of sorts and feel valued as an employee. A bonus feature is that empowered employees can help identify flaws in productivity systems. Empowered employees also help out more in high alert situations and are more productive consistently and for years to come.

Create a healthy culture - What do you imagine a healthy culture to be like in your workplace environment? Hopefully, an environment where respect, empowerment, thankfulness exist. You would be surprised how many companies overlook this main reason for successful productivity.

Positively encourage accountability - when communication contains integrity, meaning respect for the employees, genuineness, and gracious honesty, employees will respond positively and want to show respect, which generates accountability within their role. They are more prone to encourage their co-workers to do the same as they begin to work as a team. Because of clear messages delivered from upper management, employees know what is expected of them and feel that these expectations are easy to achieve. Accountability opens the path to achievement. As these achievements are praised through positive communication, employees yearn to earn more.

Remembering that positive, encouraging productive communication is free - You would think this fact alone would drive home every effort to improve productivity communication. Coming up with the right words to say does not cost any money or take more time. Once the basics of communication are put into practice, more company time will be available to help the company grow. The tried and true basics are the answer to every work-related issue. By learning the basics and putting them into practice, you will be injecting your business with the number one way to success. You will be putting the derailed train on the track that helps your company achieve the goals you envision for free.

Getting everyone behind the company's mission - Make sure to communicate your company's mission, as well as goals. Also, share your company's success. Employees like to be on a winning team, so make sure yours is one.

Giving employees as much freedom and autonomy as your company's mission and goals allow - Employees who are pushed too far beyond lead to low motivation and performance. The more employees reach the same goal using their particular gifts and talents within the company's boundaries, the more motivation and success. More companies are going towards this fact as employees dress more casually and offices use couches, stand-up desks, and whatever it takes to empower their employees and bring their talents to the table.

Challenging employees to reach their highest level of performance - While workplace autonomy is good, challenging employees within their world of talent is vital to an employee's self-perception and goals. Believe in them, what they are capable of and how far they can go. Challenge them in a motivational way to ask themselves, "Is there a more efficient way to accomplish all that my job requires?" Encourage them that, in all they do, to make sure their efforts have something to do with the company's bottom line or save their efforts for another, more personal project.

Creating an environment of transparency and feedback - Upper management can sometimes be hesitant about admitting mistakes. However, recognizing when you are wrong is crucial to building an open and transparent culture where everyone can feel free enough to be their best at work. This starts at the top. If you are a manager, admit when the course has gone off track. Some leaders believe that the higher the position, the more they must demonstrate control and always be correct. However, most successful leaders have found that the higher their position, the more they must support the employees working underneath their direction by giving them the resources they need and providing constant motivation, clarification, and knowledge.

Use constructive criticism - When it comes to an employee who needs to be redirected, constructive criticism is a helpful way of giving feedback that provides specific, actionable suggestions. Rather than providing general advice, constructive criticism offers specific recommendations on how to make positive improvements. Constructive criticism is explicit, to the point, and easy to put into action. Corrections that need to be made for successful productivity are received better when those adjustments are cushioned in positivity. Instead of "Why are you doing this?" or "You need to change," use the "Oreo" approach where you sandwich a correction between two compliments. Keep your focus on the needed adjustment and use encouraging words. Try to learn the process the employee uses for his or her method. Usually, there is something insightful to learn from this that can be adjusted.

Have a company newsletter - Make this newsletter short, captivating, and motivating. Never put reprimand employees in a newsletter or correct policies. Show company progress and how the team made this happen. The newsletter should only focus on employee value. Have another avenue for corrections.

Create an intranet channel - an intranet is a designated computer network for sharing company information. Excluding access by anyone other than company employees, policies and procedures are available, as well as budgets, permissions, the company's operational systems, and more. This is an excellent way for employees to stay connected.

Face-to-Face Interactions Also Help Increase Productivity

Employees love receiving upper management attention. Sitting at their desk or their station and having a member of upper management simply wave can go far in a worker's day to promote team effort, personal recognition, and value.

Instead of directly entering your office in the mornings, take a route that generates face-to-face contact with your employees. Simple chats or references to their favorite sports teams or that daughter-in-law who's due to have a baby any day can increase productivity morale quicker than a costly, hour-long motivational speaker.

Remember to be yourself - Employees do not like to be manipulated by phoniness or insincerity. Employees give you most of their time and effort. They expect honesty, respect, and dignity in return. You must genuinely believe in yourself, what you are trying to accomplish and what you think your employees are capable of achieving.

Know your employees - To win over your employees, you must know your employees, and not just their name. The more you know their history, the more they will feel your investment in them. This doesn't take hours of communication to develop. It merely means asking the right questions. This type of probing into what motivates them helps you to do your job more efficiently. While walking past, say hi and refer back to those points of interest you've learned about them.

Shower them with appreciation - Remember, remember, remember, employees love attention, especially in the form of gratitude. Even something that is quickly sent out in a company email. The best companies to work for are those that are filled with employee recognition.

Speak on a communication level that's easy to understand - According to quote.com, Bernie Sanders speaks on a ninth-grade level, Hillary Clinton and Taylor Swift speak at an eighth-grade level, and Stephen Colbert talks at a sixth-grade level. Never speak over an employee's head or talk down to them. Avoid using unclear words like "this, that, and it" Make sure to speak on a level that every employee understands your message. As poet William Yeats once said, "Think as a wise man but communicate in the language of the people."

As your workplace environment grows in motivation and positivity, not only will revenue increase, but employee retention will also rise. Employees who are satisfied with their jobs rarely leave, even for higher pay. The rewards for employee satisfaction cannot be overemphasized. When an employee trusts that their company values them, this becomes as real as money in their pocket. Spend as much time on employee loyalty as you do on company loyalty and watch your company soar.

Chapter Five Overview

- A business is only as successful as its employees.
- Hire the right employees first.
- Poor communication is the number one reason for project and product failures.
- Alleviate this issue by using programs like Microsoft Lync, HipChat, Bootcamp, Kato, Redbooth, Wrike, and Campfire, to name a few.

Other ways to generate maximum productivity include:
- Only communicate accurate information.
- Develop trust through open communication.
- Empower employees to become experts in their field.
- Create a healthy workplace culture.
- Positively encourage accountability.

- Remembering that positive, encouraging, productive communication is free.

Face-to-face contact with your employees includes:
- Be yourself.
- Create an environment of transparency and feedback.
- Know your employees.
- Shower your employees with appreciation.
- Get everyone behind the company's mission.
- Give your employees as much freedom and autonomy as your company's mission and goals allow.
- Speak on a communication level that's easy to understand
- Use only constructive criticism
- Have a company newsletter
- Use the intranet

Chapter Six: Effective Communication For Online Work

"Remember, not only to say the right thing in the right place, but far more difficult still, to leave unsaid the wrong thing at the tempting moment."
Benjamin Franklin

History of Online Work/Video Conferencing

Along with the 1930s inventions of sliced bread, Toll House cookies, nylon-bristled toothbrushes, Scotch tape, and the first car radio, attempts were made to create video conferencing. This came in the form of still photos, but not much more. By the 1970s, AT&T used video conferencing for its Picturephone service. Jack Nilles, a scientist from NASA communications, developed the term "telecommuting" in the early 1970s. In the 1980s, this term spread as IMB began placing "remote terminals" in their employees' homes and creating CU-SeeMe as a video conferencing tool in the 1990s. And now? Estimations are that businesses in America conduct 55 million video conferences in one week. Ninety-four percent of companies who use online conferencing claim their companies gain from increased productivity.

Online Work Communication Options

While telecommuting, remote or online work becomes more popular. Many companies continue to call off this avenue of employment as efforts to succeed in this arena fail. Productivity declines, and employee morale just isn't the same. There are things you can do to make sure your company is among the ones that flourish.

One of the main concerns of online work is how to communicate. Especially when emails, Slack, and other online messaging systems eliminate facial expressions, nonverbal cues, and tones. As mentioned in Chapter One, 7% of a message is word choice, 38% is tone, and 55% is body language. This means that we eliminate 93% of a message's impact whenever we use online messaging systems and must depend on the 7% word choice factor to convey our message correctly. Word choice becomes crucial, so we must know exactly what each word means before we use it.

Online work has its challenges. Using text-only discussions can be challenging for those who cannot spell, lack sufficient keyboard skills, and are not comfortable writing. Video conferencing can also be uncomfortable for those unfamiliar with it or who do not like being "on camera." Working from home can make employees feel isolated and disengaged.

There are those employees, and managers, who believe the only way to collaborate on a project truly is to have in-person meetings, etc. How do you keep your team engaged enough to continue to produce at maximum capacity when life factors and business preferences shift the work environment to remote work?

As with any other aspect of business success, communication will make or break remote work, as well. Staying in touch and updating as much as possible helps everyone stay on the same page and maintain employee value and cohesiveness.

How to Make Sure Your Company's Online Work Is Successful

Several steps can be taken to make sure the remote scene is thriving and does not lose anything when compared to the workplace environment:

Make communicating with your team a top priority with consistency and value - Be proactive with your employees, particularly to resolve issues immediately that slow down productivity. Morning business meetings help organize the goals of the day. The more you can stabilize your work environment and goals, particularly during unstable times, the better. Your "company" ship in any type of storm must remain on course. Morning meetings are also an excellent time to strengthen your team and help everyone feel connected.

Make sure expectations are made and understood from the beginning - Don't assume your team will all be on the same page in terms of work hours or when you should be available for check-ins and conference calls. It's essential to outline your expectations from the get-go to reduce frustration and ensure a smooth transition to the new work from home setting. As F. Scott Fitzgerald once said, "Genius is the ability to put into effect what is on your mind."

Agree on what communication preferences work best - It is vital for remote workers to be reliable and accessible any time they are on the timeclock. One employee may feel most comfortable with email, while another one might want to use Slack. Consider communicating with each employee in the way they feel most comfortable, then, after everyone feels more at ease speaking online, streamlining your communications through either a Zoom call or Google Chat might be more manageable.

Provide updates continually - Update contact information frequently to keep everyone connected. Management must convey any changes in processes or platforms, or other systems to employees before changes occur. Calendars must also remain updated to match each workday. Because of the isolation from co-workers, all employees must be kept in the loop, or confusion and then frustration is the result.

Even though your employee(s) are out of visual range, resist the urge to micromanage - With online communication, there is the urge to check in on your employees several times a day, but this can prove to be more of a hindrance than a help as your employees feel too much of a distraction. Plus, this sends a message of mistrust. Just as trust is developed in a standard workplace environment, this must also be the case with online work. Communication will be the key to creating trust, identifying mistrust, and knowing where each employee stands on the production measurement scale.

Be flexible because online work is still a work in progress - Online communication can hinder, or alter, some of the Basics of Communication. Keep this in mind as you receive each communication, and your brain works to decode the mess. Since the way we look when we speak and other body expressions play an essential part in communication, when these factors are eliminated, the written word takes on a heavier weight. The decoding of receiving a written message relies on the written word only as the tone is eliminated. Make sure the messages you send include words that create a softer tone. No capital letters and using the term "you" is too direct when used negatively. A grammar program, like Grammarly, can check for style and make sure your message is delivered in the tone you desire. Avoid costly misunderstandings by paying more attention to what you say in your written statements.

Be Careful With Humor

And remember, humor does not always, so be careful. Sometimes people may not receive your expression of humor in the way you intended.

When engaged in the written word and verbal conversations, make sure the first thought that comes to mind is screened in your mind. Communication is so fast-paced that screening words before they are spoken has almost become a lost art that carries a high liability. More and more, comments are being put under a microscope. More and more people have to apologize publicly or, even worse, step down from their positions because of something they said without filtering the comment first. Here are a few of those comments:

- Stacey Dash, known for her role in "Clueless," got herself into trouble when she appeared on The Meredith Vieira Show and commented that the difference between male and female wages was generated by women who were simply lazy and unwilling to work hard enough to receive the higher pay rate.
- Jamie Foxx also got himself into trouble at the 2015 iHeartRadio Music Awards when he commented that Bruce Jenner would be in attendance to perform a "his" and "her" duet all by himself." Not funny to his fans and others.
- FOX News television news anchor Chris Wallace once found himself needing to apologize for the unprofessional comment he made on air when he said about Kelly Clarkson, "Holy cow, did she blow up. She should stay off the deep dish pizza for a little while."

Each of us has times when we say things we shouldn't. Saying those things in a professional setting can be costly, so make sure to filter everything you say, especially when it comes to online communications.

What It Takes To Have Successful Online Employees

Every company's dream is to have fully productive online employees. And you can by following these expert tips:

Offer appropriate training to ensure successful productivity at home - Aim for success. Encourage the employee to have a healthy workplace free from their home environment where they can 100% focus on performance and results.

Establish realistic goals and expectations - Make sure to clarify employee priorities. Focus on expectations and make sure they are agreed upon in writing. Outline tasks and measurements for success.

Discuss issues - Welcome feedback. Address issues immediately. Stay on top of how remote work is affecting your employees. Should experience real frustration between you and your employees, never communicate in an emotionally charged way. Managers should handle this type of situation through a phone call or, even better, face-to-face meeting.

Stay on topic - It is easier in online discussions and meetings to stray from the subject. Online communication can feel more casual as we are used to having this form of face-to-face communication in only informal settings. Have a known agenda and make good use of this time. Remember, this is a professional setting with goals to be accomplished within each online meeting.

Offer more lead time on projects that need to be completed - Remote work happens in a different setting that can take more time for some tasks to be completed. Distractions include kids at home, pending chores, easy access to television, online shopping, video games, and more. Allowing more time for this reality is a reasonable expectation for success in this environment.

Make sure morale is still a vital goal - It would be easy to conclude that a different environment means using different approaches. While this is true, one thing that should not change is employee morale. You may have to have a different approach to morale, but a positive, cohesive company environment is still at the top of the list. Informal time with employees online is vital to include and goes far for company morale, after all necessary business is concluded. Scheduling coffeehouse meetings help boost morale, as well as holding creative online events. These include:
- Cooking classes
- Planned online games
- Virtual dance parties
- Online team-building Bingo

If your employees don't experience morale-boosting communications from you, they won't be experiencing this critical team-building angle to online work.

Address technical difficulties immediately - Take care of every technical issue as it arises. Your only line of connection to your business is now in the hands of computers and other electronic devices. Lack of support or delays on this end can kill morale.

Discuss options for reporting progress - Have an employee-friendly tracking system for all improvement, which the whole team can see. Project Web App is one platform that tracks time spent on project tasks leading towards completion. This program also tracks vacation time, sick leave, and other administrative needs, The same view or separate views can also be incorporated.

Call when necessary - the rule is usually if more than three emails are needed, a different communication avenue should be used, preferably a phone call or face-to-face meeting.
Establish a mutually agreeable time zone - If your employees are spread across different time zones, set a time zone that works for everyone's circumstances.

Consider using emojis - Sometimes, some messages are hard to decipher. When in doubt, a smiley face can help clarify tone and avoid a misunderstanding.

Over-communicate rather than under-communicate - This is where texts can fill in nicely. Texts do not invade time or space and can be read when time is available, and are easy to use to confirm all aspects of working remotely and checking in. Over-communicate, especially in the beginning, within reason, to make sure everyone is on the same page.

Do not assume anything - The old saying, "To assume makes an ASS out of U and ME," applies 100 percent to your online workplace. Because of the gaps that can arise with online employees, ensure that clarity and accuracy are consistent. If there are any misunderstandings or miscommunication, take care of them immediately, so they don't grow bigger. With online communication, containing your workplace environment is vital.

Identify, by name, who is responsible for what tasks - For example:

Good morning team,

    This morning, we'll have:

Kent will manage the Smith project.
Ashlee will oversee materials.
Brandon will communicate with the client.

    Please respond within the hour, identifying that you received this email.

Clarity is crucial. Timeframes help forward movement.

Give prompt response times - Not all teams function the same. Since we cannot be available every minute of every day, a discussion should be held regarding a reasonable response time. Talk to your team about this and come up with a response time that's agreeable for your employees' group.

Ask yourself, "What would it be like to be on the receiving end of my online communications?" This question alone can help set up your delivery. Empathy is one of the top contributors to effective communication, so always be mindful of what the other person, or people, might think about your thoughts before you even express them.

More companies are transitioning to online work. This is a work in progress, which means it could have its issues, and it could have its opportunities to pioneer this ever-expanding industry.

Chapter Six Overview

How to Make Sure Your Company's Online Work Is Successful

- Make communicating with your team a top priority with consistency and value.
- Make sure expectations are made and understood from the beginning.
- Agree on what communication preferences work best.
- Provide updates continually.
- Even though your employee(s) will be out of sight, resist the urge to micromanage.
- Be flexible with the fact that online work is still a work in progress.
- When engaged in written, verbal conversations, make sure to filter your thoughts before you communicate them.
- Offer appropriate training to ensure successful productivity at home.
- Establish realistic goals and expectations.
- Discuss any issues.
- Stay on topic.
- Offer more lead time on projects that need to be completed.
- Make sure morale is still a vital goal.

These include:
- ➢ Cooking classes
- ➢ Planned online games
- ➢ Virtual dance parties
- ➢ Online team-building Bingo
- Address technical difficulties immediately.
- Discuss options for reporting progress.
- Place a phone call when necessary.

- Establish a mutually agreeable time zone.
- Consider using emojis.
- Over-communicate rather than under-communicate.
- Do not assume anything.
- Identify, by name, who is responsible for what tasks.
- Give one another prompt response times.
- Ask yourself, "What would it be like to be on the receiving end of my online communications?"

Chapter Seven: Effective Communication For Company Growth

"Success is not final; failure is not fatal: It is the courage to continue that counts."
Winston Churchill

Communication Within An Ever-expanding Company

Only things that are alive can change and grow. So, the good news is, if your company is growing, your company is very much alive and thriving.

As a company grows, effective communication can quickly become a real issue. Phones are ringing, inboxes are full, and new products arrive. Now, more than ever, precise, rapid, accurate, and knowledgeable communications are critical. Interestingly enough, effective communication is one of the top reasons why a company soars. Yet, within this rapid growth, communication can quickly become the first factor that's forgotten or taken for granted. The result? Frustration, poor communication, and low morale.

Many CEOs lay in bed awake at night perplexed by this phenomenon. What can be done? As mentioned before, over-communicate. Make sure every employee, through the chain of command, relays messages to their department, so everyone remains on the same page.

Email even a quick hello to the company each morning with a thought, a success, and a well wish.

Communicating While Expanding Tips

When work-life becomes fast and furious, at a time when it would be easy to think that everyone can just get along while more important aspects are being taken care of, nothing could be further from the truth. Communication cannot hibernate or wait. Managers must address it every day, like food to the body, so that everyone can stay connected and updated. This means:

Don't forget what got you to the growth you're experiencing - this includes continuing to expect and then supporting solid communication from top to bottom and side to side. A lot should change, but communication shouldn't.

For a business to grow, stellar communication must remain in effect - As soon as this is established, growth will be the result. Communication must continue to be smooth to keep this momentum even though disruptions may arise as new positions are created, and current jobs may be eliminated. To gain company cohesiveness, the following proves helpful:

A proper chain of command - Employees of successfully run companies understand the overall chain of command. Once this hierarchical structure is set in place, the chain of communication becomes neat and orderly. Misunderstandings are fewer, and response times are quicker. The primary reason why a chain of command is so important is that every employee understands their responsibility for tasks that need to be completed and issues that arise. Project management software also helps support the chain of command. Trello, Basecamp, Smartsheet, and Mavenlink organize tasks, post due dates, and provide a chain of command details. Also beneficial is that many of these programs have a lot of transparency as employees can see what they are doing. Questions are more quickly and easily answered with project management software.

Consistent communication with every manager - As your successful communication programs begin to take off, continual motivation, trust, and empowerment among your managers is vital. Delegation to trusted employees who have exemplified stellar communication is critical. Never forget that your frontline workers are where the rubber meets the road and can make or break a company because of their continual contact with customers. In this way, they are the face of your company. Many companies are successful because they understand the value of frontline workers. They are usually some of the lower-paid, so, because of this, they must be incentivized with perks and other motivational actions to remind them continually of how valuable they are.

In 2016-17, Monster partnered with kununu to see what workplace factors are the most important for employee job satisfaction among some of the best places to work. Here are a few of their responses:

1. American LegalNet employees stated that communication between employees and management is always open, leading to transparency and effective workflow.
2. In-N-Out Burger states that managers must be great communicators who try to make scheduling work and shifts run smooth.
3. Barnes and Noble say that a strong emphasis is placed on communication from the top down. Managers check with staff before shifts to discuss goals.

Fill in a lot of details - Most managers' and owners' roles function a lot like an orchestra leader. "A little more trombone over there, a little less drums over here." As managers lead their teams, they must make sure each employee knows "what notes to play" for the coordinated effort to work. Communication is the only way this can work as the manager tweaks an employee's performance here and adjusts another employee's performance there. Once this happens and the whole team is in sync, the crescendo begins, and the company is ready to take off to a higher, more productive, social level. Ensure your employees know "what notes to play" by giving them all the details they need to make their job easier.

Make sure problems turn into learning opportunities - When major miscommunications happen, make sure to learn why, and then reassess to make sure this doesn't happen again. Rather than wasting time venting frustration or being shocked that such a thing would happen, acknowledge the issue, assess the problem, make the improvements needed and move on. If not, the company runs the risk of heading down a different path than attended.

A popular Smartphone of the 1980s experienced this problem. After rising to the top of the communication device industry, dialogue between upper management and the employees broke, and the result was disastrous for the company. Once boasting of a $230 share in the stock market, the shares dropped to a measly eight dollars because everyone took their eyes off the importance of internal communication.

Be assertive - To grow as a company, proactive managers must convey the right kind of communication. Being proactive is not the same as being aggressive. Being aggressive is offensive and a way to get ahead at all costs. Being assertive is being confident and decisive and should also include kindness as part of the company leader's delivery. If you are in a leadership role, know that within the necessary boundaries of workplace communication, direction must still occur. Listen, emotionally understand, and then have in mind how this conversation can genuinely line up with the company's needs.

Leaders should also continually communicate the company's goal and then translate those words into action- With different employees having different roles, managers must remind them all of the company's mutual goals that everyone shares.

During times of company growth, successful communication should be found most among the leaders of the company. They are the beacon to which employees look for intellectual, financial, and emotional direction.

During times of growth, it can be more difficult to communicate within the workplace. New strategies may have to be created to help address the growing needs as employees hurry to keep up.

Hold company-wide meetings - Possibly, you'll need to hold company-wide meetings at times to make sure everyone hears the same vital messages. These will have to be well-thought-out to make sure the most critical topics remain the most important topics. And then, they must be delivered in a way that engages an audience. Make sure to have an agenda and consider having break-out sessions for gatherings within each department to meet their unique needs.

Encourage two-way communication -Two-way communication is one way of the best ways to guarantee your employees feel involved in a growing company. Create a process where employees can share their successes, tips, and concerns. Any time employees are given a voice, they feel acknowledged and of value.

Have a Communications Director - Depending on the company's size, sometimes a communication director is hired.

Make sure this person is someone everyone respects, or the effort will backfire. This person works as the liaison between upper management and employees.

Use an internal database for all pertinent information - In a company that has grown exponentially, make sure to have an internal database that captures company processes, plans, essential messages, and other factors that, if needed, employees can go back and search through.

The cost of neglecting stellar communication is steep. Nothing kills morale more than frustrated managers, and the following will result:

Lack of proper employee knowledge base - when this happens, you can kiss your company goodbye. Nothing frustrates an employee more than not having what they need to do their job promptly, including all necessary information. Often, more employees than are required must now focus on one project. Lack of knowledge can also become a risk to a company as misunderstandings lead to costly mistakes.

Emotionally neglected employees - starved to have their emotional cups restored, employees become emotionally drained and stop caring about all that was once so important to them. When this happens, poor quality, or no quality work, is the result. And why not? If management doesn't care, why should we?

Unnecessary conflict - This wastes so much company time that company revenue now decreases as more and more time is directed towards conversations and actions that are not directed towards productivity. Employees who are under stress cannot perform at the top of their game.

Conflict spreads - When tension is high, this spreads like wildfire, gossip begins, disgruntled employees emerge, and effectiveness and productivity in the workplace are seriously affected.

Mistrust develops - mistrust is the enemy of cohesiveness. A lack of communication in the workplace means the transmission doesn't stop. It's just headed in the wrong direction. For example, employees who see co-workers being fired without company explanation. Most employees develop bonds with their co-workers and learn to create their own team when management won't. Having one of their own let go can kill morale. Equally as important is an opportunity for advancement that arises, and current employees are not notified. This sends the message that upper management is continually seeking better talent because the current employees are not good enough to be considered.

The result of all this is the company's cancer: low morale. Once this happens, even more time is spent on damage recovery, if this is even possible. Remember the cellular company of the 1980s that went from being the number one product to nearly invisible because of company miscommunication?

Seventy percent of employees feel stressed because of ineffective communication in the workplace, found Dynamic Signal, an employee communication, and engagement company. The same study found that 80% of the American workforce claims ineffective communication is the cause. This same company found that 80 percent of the U.S. workforce is under stress, stating ineffective communication is the cause. Sixty-three percent say they want to quit their job because poor communication interrupts their ability to perform.

Poor communication costs $62.4 million annually for the average company. No company can afford this. First, you must have your product or service, and then next, you must have a dynamite team to support it. All resources should go towards making sure your most significant resource is functioning at their highest level. They are the ones who will get you to the top.

A lot has changed in workplace communication, with millennials preferring digital communication over notes, posters, and meetings. Adapt to the times, or your company will suffer. Different styles of transmission are high on the list for communication failures. Do not set up a system without finding out what works in your specific employee environment.

Just remember to make communication during growth a top priority. Weave this vital step in company growth into the fabric of your culture. By expecting, and then supporting, healthy communication from the top, growing companies will continue to attract and retain the stellar kind of talent needed to sustain all the growth.

Chapter Seven Overview

Like food for the body, communication must be a constant factor. To main company cohesiveness, the following proves helpful:

- A proper chain of command.
- Consistent communication with every manager.
- Fill in a lot of details.
- Make sure problems turn into learning opportunities.
- Be assertive.
- Leaders should also continually communicate the company's goals and then translate those words into action.
- Hold company-wide meetings.

- Encourage two-way communication.
- Have a Communications Director.
- Use an internal database for all pertinent information.

Neglecting employees through poor communication results in:

- Lack of proper employee knowledge base.
- Emotionally neglected employees.
- Unnecessary conflict.
- Mistrust develops.

To recover:
- Make communication during growth a top priority.

Chapter Eight: Effective Communication For Stellar Management

Communication Begins With Upper Management

According to a Harvard Business Review survey, fifty-eight percent of people trust strangers more than they believe their boss. A recent Gallup poll found that 50 % of employees quit their jobs solely because of their manager. Being an owner or a manager means carrying the heavyweight of responsibility to ensure a company heads towards success. And what is their most incredible tool? Communication.

Here's an example of a poor manager paraphrased from themuse.com after they requested submissions for horrible managers:

There was an employee who had a boss. In weekly meetings, his boss would randomly choose one employee to be the company's hero for the week. The boss would then select another employee to be the loser. The loser never did anything right and could bring the team and maybe even the whole company down. "We're talking full-on harassment in front of a crowd," the employee said.

This employee claimed that the employees never knew what was going on or if they would be called out to be the next victim. This made it so that every employee dreaded going to this meeting.

"Once you knew you weren't going to be the employee that was chosen to be the loser of the week, you could relax."

But then, he went on to say that the employees would all feel bad for the employee that was selected, especially if you were chosen to be the hero. There never was any reason an employee was selected to be the loser or the hero, this was just management's style.

Most employees remember two types of managers: the best ones and the worst ones. The best are never forgotten because of all they did to improve the employee's experience at work and change their life for the better. Since so much time is spent at work, to have a fantastic boss makes all of life more manageable as one makes an employee feel better, not only about their job but about who they are as a person and the daily work they put in. The worst ones never listen, accuse, do not understand, and eventually deflate an employee completely. Be the best manager or employee you can, and success opportunities will continue to open up for you.

Another employee tells the story of a boss who just doesn't get it when it comes to workplace communication:

This employee was employed at a company that rotated their employees to various projects under different directions. One of the managers was the worst, the employee claimed.

"He would interrupt me while I was intensely focused on a project and ask aggressively, "How is everything going?"

If the employee were slow at answering because her primary concentration was on her project and she was deeply involved in various Excel rows and columns, he'd say, "Are you nervous? You sure seem like it. Is everything going okay? Are you sure? Why did you select that word over there?"

The employee later learned that this manager was a former interrogator. How do you think his managerial style contributed to the company's goal of high morale?

Tips For Upper Management

Establish as early as possible a solid baseline communication standard. This is accomplished by:

Evaluating your current workplace communication process - Evaluate your company as a whole and where communication stands on your list. Prioritize your list, making sure to put internal communication near the top, then ask:

- What are your company communication goals?
- What is your current internal communication process?
- How is this process working out for you?
- What improvements need to be made to reach your goals of continual written and verbal interaction with your team?
- Consider all forms of communication within the company: employee-to-employee, manager-to-employee, etc.

When planning your internal communication process:

Consider your team - think about all the employees within your company for whom this communication system is considered. Break the organization down into teams. What are their goals, history, and preferences for receiving messages and direction? Consider their mindsets and how they can become engaged in the communication process.
Identify best strategies - Determine what steps need to be completed to achieve the goals above.

Assign tasks - After completing the tasks, compare your new system with the goals you set and make sure they are met. Every new system brings change. Employees do not like change, and this dialogue will have to be held to help them understand that the changes will make their workload easier (and this better be the case).

Offer reassurance - Management should reassure that this change is worth it and was made with the employees in mind. This is a time when opposing teams could emerge as an "us," and "them" mentality possibly emerges. It is your job to calm these waters with continual encouragement, listening, empathy for their cause, validation of their importance within the company. That effort is being made to stabilize the situation and have the new system in place as soon as possible.

Orient employees - The earlier, the better. Making employees feel included will help them buy-in. As part of your plan, make sure that you enlist the support of owners and managers first. When employees sense hesitation on the part of upper management, they will follow this response. This is where division can arise, stall the effort, and waste time. The administration should not only endorse the chosen system but also hype it up, continue, and genuinely present the benefits.

Not every employee will embrace the primary communication system selected for your internal communication, making it essential to consider options. Fortunately, communicating the same message across multiple platforms is easy to integrate the many available software programs.

Consider remote workers - Communicating with remote employees might differ from your in-house workers. Locating the right technology for this type of fit is possible and crucial. Make sure to ask for feedback from remote employees and even ask around for what their thoughts might be. Most employees, if asked, have an answer to their job assignment issues. This is because, while working, especially during times of frustration, they usually say to themselves, "If only I had... to complete my task or communicate or any other issues that might arise.

Listen - the number one tool to strengthen your internal communication is to listen to your employees to the point of absorbing their ideas. Even if you never use them, this still makes the employee feel valued. Listening starts at the top, so no matter your role in the company, you need to set the example and listen.

Cloud collaboration - Cloud-based programs are a genius answer to everyday company issues: saving and sharing documents. Internal documents are the meat and potatoes of a company and must be easily acceptable. Again, this is one more resource that makes an employee's job easier.

Tips For Great Management Communication

Managerial Do's

Do be a great manager - Great managers oversee, provide and coordinate. They do the things employees can't do, while employees do all the rest of the things a task needs to be completed. Make sense? Managers think, help, prepare, make and share critical decisions, and implement friendly organizational structures that everyone can depend on.

Do Praise often - this goes without saying. Praise is the fuel that gets the rocket soaring. Praise good work, don't take it for granted. Public recognition and acknowledgment inspire loyalty and increases motivation, engagement, and general happiness. Share your appreciation in team meetings, emails, and don't forget to include those praiseworthy points in performance reviews.

Do check for updates, but don't micromanage – Develop a routine for updating all tasks delegated out, either through a 5-minute standup meeting each morning or through an email checklist or even a software program for task completion. You will know, by how people respond, who are the real taskmasters. Taskmasters love updating because of all they have accomplished. Employees who are behind are always filled with excuses.

President Theodore Roosevelt, the 26th President of the United States, said it best:

> "The best executive is the one who has sense enough to pick good men
> to do what he wants done,
> and self-restraint to keep from meddling while they do it."

Do be clear and concise when describing a task – Make sure you know precisely how to explain a task before delegating it out. Outlining the task in list form can help. Include the task, the resources, the expectations, and the timeframe.

Managerial Don'ts

Do not personally criticize - When problems arise, direction is needed or more training, but personal attacks are not professional, and managers can lose all respect on this point alone.

Do not hold lengthy meetings just to hear yourself speak – poor managers love to hear themselves talk and create as many opportunities as they can for this to happen. Employees want to be heard, too, for all the effort they put in. Employees usually know more than managers when it comes to where the rubber meets the road. Managers who don't listen, but talk, talk, talk often must post on Indeed for employees needed.

Do not use disciplinary write-ups to motivate your employees to do their job – this seems like a given, but poor managers believe they hold the power to say all and do all. One of the worst forms of "motivation" is to have words spread that the manager is disciplinary-form-happy. This kills morale, establishes morale as something found at the bottom of a sad barrel, and takes the air out of even the most stellar of employees' sails. Oprah Winfrey once said, "You usually get that which you fear the most." If you fear having a poor work ethic and run on this platform, you will usually get a poor work ethic from your employees.

Do not speak in code – when you talk to your employees, do not speak vaguely. Speak clearly and even, sometimes, directly, as to what needs to be accomplished. Employees want clarity to know exactly what to do because they know when their task is completed, and they can reap the rewards of a great job well done.

Do not be a terrible listener – employees despise managers who forget to bring their ears to work. Look at your employee as he or she speaks to you. Repeat back some of the words you hear. Always listen more than you talk.

Do not make a decision, and then ask for input – employees detest being called away from their desk to be asked for input on a specific situation, only to have their boss summarize and never include a word the employee said. Especially when the manager asks for input, the employees are excited to give it, and then the manager, while wrapping up, never mentions any words the employees offered but sticks to his or her original plan.

Do not ignore wants, needs, and complaints – for an employee to go to a manager with a complaint is usually not the norm, so when it happens, it must be for a legitimate reason. Maybe resources are low, the room is too hot, one of the employees is not pulling their load. Usually, these conversations take place because the employee is at the end of their rope. And then, to have this communication ignored is demoralizing, frustrating, and can even render the best employee to become useless. If management doesn't care, why should I?

Do not withhold important information – vital information, not passed along, makes the team feel like, for all the work they do, their efforts do not matter. There is no team without that team having all the information they need to do their job, particularly topics like the owner is coming, there is a meeting, or a particular software program is broken. Employees need to be updated to do their job effectively. And most employees want to excel in their position.

Pleasing Employees

While you're trying to be everything for everybody, remember that you can't please all of the employees all of the time, but you can always be nice.

There is an old fable that shows this nicely called, *The Miller, His Son And The Ass*:

> There was once a miller who had a son. One day, while taking their ass to sell at the market, they passed a group of young ladies who laughed at how silly the miller was because he had an ass to sit upon, and yet he was walking. So, the miller picked up his son and placed him on the ass's back. The miller and his son continued to walk to the market. As they did, they came upon some old folks. Believing the miller was crazy, they clearly told him that he should never allow his son to ride the ass when he should be the one to benefit from the relief the ass would provide. The miller removed his son from the ass's back and climbed upon the ass. The miller and the son traveled on down the road when they passed a

group of travelers. The travelers told the miller that if he wanted to sell the ass, the miller and his son should carry the ass, or the ass would become exhausted and worthless. The miller and his son took the ass's legs and bound them to a pole. Together the miller and his son carried the ass. When they approached the town where the market was held, the townspeople laughed at the sight of the miller and his son. Their laughter was so loud that the noise frightened the ass, who then kicked himself away from the miller and his son, then fell off a bridge and drowned. The horrified and embarrassed miller and his son went home with nothing but the knowledge that if you try to please everyone, you might be the one who ends up sad.

Denial In The Workplace

Yes, you can't please everyone. And remember, denial is a wonderful place for the denying person to be, but his or her actions make a lot more work for everyone around him or her.

This truth can be pervasive in the workplace and slow down the company as well. Make sure when this happens that healthy discussions take place and reality checks abound.

Our Ever-changing World And How Communication Fits In

Fortunately, our world is continually becoming more and more diverse. This grants us new opportunities for new awareness, new processes, all leading to a better world. No longer do we do things the same way, except when it comes to communication basics. Our history led to our current status, which then leads to the context for new conversations. New awareness leads to better understanding.

How fortunate we are to each be able to dream and have visions for a better life. All of this needs new products and services to help support our efforts.

We are also a world where miscommunication is much more costly. We run to Google and are too quick to conclude when it comes to the happenings around us. Communication is all about listening, pausing to understand. This all applies to the workplace also.

To show the power of words and the power of understanding, a friend who works in an assisted living community tells the story of this assisted living community's builders. They decided to include a technology room where they could store all their electronic equipment. They thought it would be fun and progressive to name this room "The Brain Room."

When the building opened, a female resident who was a former policewoman moved in. One day, after walking past The Brain Room, the former cop approached my friend with fear and trepidation.

"Can I talk to you?" she muttered, shaking to the core.

"Of course," said the employee.

"Could you please get rid of that room upstairs? It terrifies me."

"What room?" said the employee as she thought of all the beautiful rooms in that brand new building.

In tears, the woman said, "The Brain Room. I do not want them to do brain control on me. I won't have it. No, I won't. No one's going to take control of my brain."

The builders never anticipated that their "fun and progressive" word choice would translate into a horror statement to an older generation who had their interpretation of what these words meant.

By following all the steps in this book, especially The Basics of Communication, you will have every tool you need to be the most effective manager ever.

Chapter Eight Overview
Facts regarding managers:
- Fifty-eight percent of people trust strangers more than they believe their boss,
- 50 % of employees quit their jobs solely because of their manager
- Most employees remember two types of managers: the best ones and the worst ones.

Tips For Upper Management
- Establish as early as possible a strong baseline communication standard
- Evaluate your current workplace communication process
- Consider your team
- Assign tasks
- Offer reassurance
- Orient employees
- Consider remote workers
- Listen
- Cloud collaboration

By following all the steps in this book, especially The Basics of Communication, you will have every tool you need to be the most effective manager ever.

Conclusion

Communication Is A Complicated Art, Science, and Liability

As a review, remember, communication is now a complicated art, science, and liability, especially in the workplace. Understanding its full spectrum is vital. Every word must be delivered and received with great understanding, sensitivity and accuracy.

Quality workplace correspondence relies on various factors, including accuracy, staff engagement, and sufficient information message. Our choice of words and how we say them can make or break our workplace relationships and opportunities. Essential communication means assessing your current style of workplace communication, understanding the basics, then adjusting your

Too many owners, upper management, and employees believe communication is just exchanging thoughts and opinions. Yet, there is so much more to communicating with your employees. Continuous variables go along with each word we speak. No two conversations are ever the same. Essential communication can take ordinary employees to extraordinary places.

One of the most significant changes in recent decades has been in the ways Americans communicate. As the world becomes more connected through social networking, communication becomes more vital. Communication has now, more than ever, become a crucial tool to survival and co-existence.

The other reason why effective communication is so important is that we live in an ever-changing of verbal and written exchanges. As we move forward in a more fast-paced world, electronic devices continue to speed up the process of disseminating information in the most effective way possible.

There's More To Communication Than Just Words
Today more than ever, what you say is the number one factor influencing how others feel about you and the capabilities you possess. One of the most critical aspects of communication is having empathy for everyone you converse with. Remember? This means feeling the conversation from their perspective as well as yours. One way to develop instant empathy with the other person you are speaking to is to ask questions to understand the other person first.

Another critical factor to remember is that the words we speak and hear are often cushioned in words that help others receive our message. This is where the all-important phrase came from, "Taken out of context." The entire context must be considered when we put together our message or decode another person's message. If a person uses one word alone, the message most likely will be distorted. Context can either clear up a misunderstanding or confuse it.

Always keep in mind that nonverbal communication comprises an endless variety of behaviors, from a smile, a frown, a scowl, a nod, the shaking of one's head, hands on hips, a wink, two thumbs up, or even a combination of these, to name a few. Keep distance in mind as well.

By reading all the cues involved in the communication, you will determine how to fit in appropriately. Mutual consideration is so important, as both the sender and the receiver pay as much attention to one another as they do to their contribution.

Expand Your Communication Experience
Expand your vocabulary. This is necessary to relate to a broader audience. Moving forward, trends include having more critical, tactical conversations that include more meaningful and productive messages.

As mentioned, communication has evolved through the centuries: From smoke signals to worldwide electronic devices. Making connections with anyone anywhere, including the workplace, means understanding the timeless and universal communication basics.

To have successful workplace communication, we must assess our current style of expressing ourselves, refresh ourselves with the communication basics and apply these changes to our relationships and contacts.

So, how do we make sure our words are adaptable at work and with anyone you meet? Think before you speak. Effective communicators are known for opening up new thoughts and feelings for the sake of new awareness and understanding.

Every person is filled with stories, and it is your job to discover them. That is one of the most significant human connections, whether this is in the workplace, at home, or with friends. These conversations may not change the world, but they are essential parts of our life as we try to stay connected.

Being Understood While Understanding Others
Communication is about making your most important messages understood. The process of communication is exciting as you choose the most precise, most accurate words you know to convey your message. You determine the pace and the tone. Take on the

challenge of making your message easy for the receiver to receive and interpret correctly.

Take on the other challenge of voice volume. Unless the person you speak to is hard of hearing or a fire has erupted, pay attention to the volume around you and adjust yours to equal or work under what you hear. Speaking at the right volume can be learned.

And pay attention to the emphasis you give your words while speaking. A talk show host once had a family on his show who was in distress for many reasons. They asked to be on the show so the host could help them resolve their issues. After listening to the family for the hour, the host said he didn't see any real problems other than word choice and tone. Their volumes were too loud, and their word choices were too extreme.

The pace is so important. Have you ever exchanged words with someone who spoke painfully slow or maniacally fast? Both extremes negate the whole communication process because both approaches are so disruptive to the coding process the brain needs to decipher the messages being received. When it comes to pace, where does the responsibility most often rest? On the shoulders of both the sender and the receiver of the message.

Communication Is The Life Blood Of A Company
Communication in the workplace is the lifeblood of the company. Poor internal workplace communication can negatively impact a company with low morale and high employee turnover. Adding to the difficulty is the fact that poor communication affects new employee attraction.

Get in the loop by knowing that more and more companies are switching to mobile communication, like Google workplace and

Slack. These programs are also very effective for those who work remotely, freelance, or are contract-based.

Do not fall into the trap that so many companies do, where they focus on external strategies for their customers yet neglect to develop their internal communication strategy. Remember: the poorer the quality of communication is within a company, the more inferior the quality of communication is with its customer.

Consider what your current internal communication processes are and if they are working. Sometimes tools that once worked become outdated as life progresses. After establishing the most effective internal communication system for your employees, continue to build on vital, positive employee interactions. Never forget the importance of casual conversation in the workplace. Not only do you learn about possible valuable personnel resources, but casual conversation also brings the team together. Employees who know each other are more likely to help out when the going gets tough.

Tough conversations are also an expected piece of the company. Make sure that even these conversations are as positive as possible. Remember, it's okay to be frustrated. It is not okay to convey this in a disrespectful way.

The Necessity Of High Morale In The Workplace
The beauty of communication allows each company's "emotional environment" to reflect a certain morale. When employees feel good about themselves and the job they are doing, management has succeeded in doing its job establishing and maintaining positive morale. Employees love feeling part of a winning team. When morale is high, employees enjoy going to work and be part of this type of momentum. Set your employees up for success from day one.

Great company leaders allow employees' unique talents to create morale that is empowering during both good and challenging times. This naturally increases employee engagement and productivity. Effective managers don't demand high performance. They put value in people, discover their talents, then seek opportunities to utilize those strengths.

In a 2016 study by BBC Lab UK, Professor Andrew Lane, his colleagues, and 44,000 participants tested certain mindsets to see which one was most effective when it came to motivation to complete a task. Inner dialogue, inner processes, imagery, and if-then scenarios were introduced to the participants. Internal dialogue, such as, "I can do this!" proved to be the most beneficial. You are the one to implant these thoughts into your employee's heads, so they can develop an "I can do this!" inner dialogue at work.

Famous businessman Richard Branson is a huge promoter that a business is only as successful as its employees. The right employees must be hired first, with primary consideration given to their ability to positively and actively engage in productive dialogue.

Keep in mind that employees cannot begin or complete a task without upper management direction to ensure expectations are met. You will do your employees a fantastic service by implementing a communication-friendly service. And don't hesitate to obtain input from your employees. Most employees want to complete their tasks but lack the necessary resources to do so.

Trust generates an environment of shared support, and this is where productivity flourishes. Solid workplace communication is the best solution for eliminating micromanaging.

Necessary Workplace Factors
It's often said that knowledge is power. This is especially true with employee productivity. Employees love not only knowing what they are doing but why they are carrying out their duties. This always helps them feel like their tasks are part of a winning process and not just something they have to cross off their list of responsibilities for the day.

What do you imagine a healthy culture to be like in your workplace environment? Hopefully, an environment where respect, empowerment, and thankfulness exist. You would be surprised how many companies overlook this main reason for successful productivity.

When workplace communication contains integrity, meaning respect for the employees, genuineness, and gracious honesty, employees will respond positively and want to show respect, which generates accountability within their role. Accountability opens the path to achievement. As these achievements are praised through positive communication, employees yearn to earn more.

By learning the basics and putting them into practice, you will be injecting your business with the number one way to success. You will be putting the derailed train on the track that helps your company achieve the goals you envision. And when you look back, you will see that all it took was something that was free.

Make sure to communicate your company's mission, as well as goals. Also, share your company's success. Employees like to be on a winning team, so make sure yours is one they can be proud of. And giving employees as much freedom and autonomy as your company's mission and goals allow. The more employees can reach the same goal using their unique gifts and talents, the more motivation and success.

While workplace autonomy is good, challenging employees within their world of talent is also vital to an employee's self-perception and your company's goals. Believe in them, what they are capable of, and watch how far they can go.

Admitting when you are wrong is crucial to building a transparent culture where everyone can feel free enough to be their best self at work. This has to start at the top, so if you're a CEO or manager, learn to admit when the course has gone a little off track.

Putting Your Employees First
Employees give you most of their time and effort. They expect honesty, respect, and dignity in return. To win over your employees, you must know your employees, and not just their name. The more you know their history, the more they will feel your investment in them. This doesn't take hours of communication to develop, it merely means asking the right questions.

Remember, remember, remember, employees love attention, especially in the form of appreciation. Even one that is quickly sent out in a company email. The best companies to work for are those that are filled with employee recognition.

As your workplace environment grows in motivation and positivity, not only will revenue increase, but employee retention will also rise. Employees who are satisfied with their jobs rarely leave, even for higher pay.

Online Work Dynamics
One of the main concerns of online work is how to communicate successfully. Especially when emails, Slack, and other online messaging systems eliminate facial expressions, nonverbal cues, and tones.

Online work has its challenges. Discussions can be challenging for those who cannot spell, lack sufficient keyboard skills, or are not comfortable writing. Working from home can also make employees feel isolated and disengaged. How do you keep your team engaged enough to continue to produce at maximum capacity when life factors and business preferences shift the work environment to remote work? Staying in touch and updating as much as possible helps everyone stay on the same page and maintain employee value and cohesiveness.

Be proactive with your employees, particularly to resolve issues immediately that slow down productivity. Your "company" ship in any type of storm must remain on course.

Remote workers need to be reliable and accessible any time that they are on the timeclock. Calendars must also remain updated to match each workday. Because of the isolation from co-workers, all employees must be kept in the loop about all changes or confusion, and then frustration is the result.

And remember, humor does not always win, so be careful. Sometimes employees may not receive your expression of humor in the way you intended. More and more people are being put under a microscope and having to apologize publicly or, even worse, step down from their position because of something they said without filtering the comment first. Each of us say things we shouldn't at times. Saying those things in a professional setting can be costly, so make sure to filter everything you say, especially when it comes to online communications.

Every company's dream is to have fully productive online employees. Aim for success. Encourage the employee to have a healthy workplace free from their home environment where they can 100% focus on performance and results. Stay on top of how remote work is affecting your employees. Online communication can feel more casual as we are used to having this form of face-to-face communication in only informal settings. Remote work happens in a different environment that can take more time for some tasks to be completed. While time changes and products and services do, too, employee morale never should.

Move With The Times
Only things that are alive can change and grow. Make sure your company is growing, and your expanding forms of communication are right there along with it. Again, interestingly enough, effective communication is one of the top reasons why a company soars. Yet, within this rapid growth, communication is usually the first factor that's forgotten. No matter what, make sure every employee, through the chain of command, relays messages to their department, so everyone remains on the same page.

Communication cannot hibernate or wait. It must be addressed every day, like food to a hungry body, so that everyone can stay connected and updated.

The primary reason why a chain of command is so important is that every employee understands their responsibility for tasks that need to be completed and issues that arise. As your successful communication programs begin to take off, delegation to trusted employees who have exemplified stellar communication is vital.

Many companies are successful because they understand the value of frontline workers.

Keep in mind that most managers' and owners' roles function a lot like an orchestra leader. "A little more trombone over there, a little fewer drums over here." As managers lead their teams, they must make sure each employee knows "what notes to play" for the coordinated effort to work. Communication is the only way this can function as the manager tweaks an employee's performance and adjusts another employee's performance. Once this happens and the whole team is in sync, the crescendo begins, and the company is ready to take off to increased revenue.

When major miscommunications happen, make sure to learn why and then reassess to make sure this doesn't happen again. Rather than wasting time venting frustration or being shocked that such a thing would happen, acknowledge the issue, assess the problem, make the improvements needed and move on. If not, the company runs the risk of heading down a different path than attended.

To grow as a company, assertive managers must convey the right kind of communication. Being proactive is not the same as being aggressive. Being aggressive is offensive and a way to get ahead at all costs. Being assertive is being confident and decisive.

During times of company growth, employees should find successful communication most among the leaders of the company. They are the beacon to which employees look for intellectual, financial, and emotional direction.

Poor communication costs $62.4 million annually for the average company. No company can afford this. First, you must have your product or service, and then next, you must have a dynamite team to support it. All resources should go towards making sure your greatest resource is functioning at its highest level.

A lot has changed in workplace communication, with millennials preferring digital communication over notes, posters and meetings. Adapt to the times, or your company will suffer. Just remember to make communication during growth a top priority. By expecting, and then supporting, healthy communication from the top, growing companies will continue to attract and retain the stellar kind of talent needed to sustain all the growth.

Memorable Managers
Most employees remember two types of managers: the best ones and the worst ones. The best are never forgotten because of all they did to not only improve the employee's experience at work but to change their life for the better.

When planning your internal communication process, think about all the employees within your company, not just upper management. Making employees feel included will help them buy-in. Make sure to ask for feedback from remote employees and even ask around for what their thoughts might be.

The number one tool to strengthen your internal communication is to listen. Listening starts at the top.

In all that you do, remember to be the memorable asset your company depends on and that this begins with effective communication in the workplace.

If you enjoyed this book, please let me know your thoughts by leaving a short review on Amazon.

www.ingramcontent.com/pod-product-compliance
Lightning Source LLC
Chambersburg PA
CBHW071420210526
45465CB00001B/463